"Kudos to Badley and Van Brummelen for this practical collection of meditations on metaphor in the classroom . . . If metaphors operate at a fundamental level of cognition, then the challenge is to intentionally choose which metaphors I employ as an educator, since they will both direct my behavior and lead to new perspectives."

—DEBORAH C. BOWEN,
Redeemer University College

"Metaphors have long been recognized as playing a key role in the ways we approach teaching and learning. The authors contributing to this book offer a thought-provoking, faith-sensitive, and a refreshingly personal guide to this important area of reflection."

—DAVID I. SMITH,
Calvin College

"Too often as teachers we worry about the words we are using and forget to pay attention to what we are actually saying to our pupils through our practice. In this innovative book Ken Badley and Harro Van Brummelen have brought together essays which help us to distinguish these. By focusing on the metaphors that shape our work, they have provided a resource that will have a significant impact on our classrooms."

—TREVOR COOLING,
Canterbury Christ Church University, UK

Metaphors We Teach By

Metaphors We Teach By

How Metaphors Shape What We Do in Classrooms

Edited by

Ken Badley and Harro Van Brummelen

WIPF & STOCK · Eugene, Oregon

METAPHORS WE TEACH BY
How Metaphors Shape What We Do in Classrooms

Wipf and Stock
An Imprint of Wipf and Stock Publishers
199 W. 8th Ave., Suite 3
Eugene, OR 97401

www.wipfandstock.com

ISBN: 978-1-62032-014-3

The editors wish to acknowledge the following for permission to publish the following material.

The editors of the journal *Canadian Children*, for permission to include (as chapter 7) a revised version of Allyson Jule's "Princesses in the Classroom: Young Children Learning to be Human in a Gendered World," which appears in the Fall, 2011 issue of that journal (Volume 36, Issue 2).

The Association of Christian schools International (ACSI, Colorado Springs, Colorado) and Purposeful Design Publishing for permission to include (in Chapter 6) material that appeared in Harro Van Brummelen's *Walking with God in the Classroom* (2009).

Some Biblical passages cited from the *New Revised Standard Version Bible*, copyright 1989, Division of Christian Education of the National Council of the Churches of Christ in the United States of America (New York). Used by permission. All rights reserved.

Some Biblical passages cited from the *New International Version of the Bible*. Copyright © 1978 by Zondervan Publishing (Grand Rapids, Michigan). Used by permission of Zondervan.

Contents

List of Contributors

Ken Badley teaches courses in philosophy of education, ethics, and faith/learning in the doctoral program at George Fox University. Ken lives in Tacoma, Washington by way of Regina, Saskatchewan; Edmonton, Alberta; and Toronto, Ontario. Ken is author of *Worldviews: The Challenge of Choice*.

Elaine Brouwer directs Alta Vista, whose mission is to support Christian schools in such areas as curriculum, assessment, professional development, collaborative learning, and school renewal. Elaine is involved in the *Spaces Where Learners Flourish* project, which means to help educators reflect on the kinds of learning spaces in which learners will flourish.

Monika Hilder teaches English at Trinity Western University in Langley, British Columbia, with professional interests in gender and spirituality, children's literature, fantasy literature, and moral education. She is the author of *Educating the Moral Imagination through Fantasy Literature: A Study in George MacDonald, C.S. Lewis, and Madeleine L'Engle*.

Jaliene Hollabaugh has completed her doctorate in education at George Fox University and formerly taught Health and P.E. at Jesuit High School in Portland, Oregon. Her professional interests include the induction of novice teachers and the role of advanced education degree programs in the professional development of teachers.

Allyson Jule teaches Education at Trinity Western University in Langley, British Columbia. She is the author of *A Beginner's Guide to Language and Gender* and *Gender, Participation and Silence in the Language Classroom: Sh-shushing the Girls*.

List of Contributors

Carla Nelson directs the Bachelor of Education program at Tyndale University College in Toronto, Ontario. Before launching into teacher preparation, she had assignments as teacher, guidance counselor and administrator in public and private schools in Saskatchewan, Alberta and Ontario. As well, Carla has had over a decade's involvement with teacher professional development in the Machakos District of Kenya.

Harro Van Brummelen is Professor Emeritus of Education at Trinity Western University in Langley, British Columbia. Harro is the author of such titles as *Telling the Next Generation: Educational Development in North American Calvinist Christian schools, Walking with God in the Classroom* and *Steppingstones to Curriculum,*

Tim Wineberg is a parishioner at St. Helen's Catholic Church in Burnaby, British Columbia, and is a former Assistant Professor of Education at Trinity Western University. Tim is author of *Professional Care and Vocation: Cultivating Ethical Sensibilities in Teaching.*

one

Metaphors: Unavoidable, Influential, and Enriching

Ken Badley and Harro Van Brummelen

IMAGINE THIS ORDINARY NOON-HOUR scene in a high school staff room. Two teachers are discussing a student whom they both teach this semester. Kevin, who teaches biology, says, "I don't know what is going on but Amanda has certainly struggled in my class the last two months. She can't seem to grasp some of the basic concepts that she will need to get through upcoming units in the course." Joan, who teaches social studies, responds, "I am actually surprised by what you've said. In my class, she's the top student and is always digging below the surface to find deeper meaning." Kevin, visibly taken aback, replies, "That's a shock; I'd gotten the impression that Amanda was close to dropping out of school."

Across the lunchroom, two other teachers discuss students in general. Megan claims that the school's proper job is to accompany children on their journey. "Each of them is headed somewhere," she states, "Our job is to watch in wonder, and to nudge and channel them where we think it appropriate to do so." Brian asks, "But can't *accompany* also mean to play a piano while the student sings or plays a musical instrument?" "Yes, it does mean that, but that's not what I'm thinking of when I use the word; I mean more like walking beside, keeping company." "But that's a cop out, it seems to me," Brian replies, "Society wants schools to equip children to function in a competitive global economy, and that requires structured, direct instruction."

No teachers may ever have spoken these exact words. However, conversations like these happen every day in school staff rooms. Teachers

1

continually say sentences filled with metaphors. The conversations contain a gold mine of educational metaphors. When a teacher speaks about a student *struggling* in class, we wonder if that means a military struggle, an athletic struggle, a political struggle or a spiritual struggle? Likely the teacher is referring to a cognitive struggle, where the student makes a great but unsuccessful effort to understand. Do we consider the language of *cognitive struggle* to be simply descriptive or do we recognize it as a metaphor, perhaps so common and therefore deeply buried that we never noticed it before as such?

Notice some other key terms in those initial conversations. What about *grasp*? Do we recognize the origins of *grasp* in the physical world, as something one might do with one's hands. Do we recognize the metaphor when we talk about someone's *getting through* a unit? What about *top student*? We have used *top* and *bottom* for so long that we no longer notice either the metaphoric character of these terms or their power. In fact, we may find ourselves resisting the claim that *top* and *bottom* are metaphoric at all. After all, how would we compare scholastic, athletic, musical, economic and other kinds of performance except with such language? We will return to these metaphors of place and orientation later.

Dropping out, another unnoticeable phrase in contemporary educational language, first appeared in 1896 (Dorn & Johanningmeier, 1999). Students undoubtedly dropped out of school before 1896 and educators undoubtedly had language to describe their doing so. We want to point to the metaphoric status of that phrase, something many may never have thought of before our noting it just now. In fact, most of the metaphors which we have peppered through the first fictional conversation above have become part of our ordinary educational lexicon. Educators do not typically think of these words and phrases as figurative language. Rather, we view them as plain language. In doing so, we lend credence to what we will call *the strong view* of metaphor—that metaphors are not just ornaments added on to literal language to help make explanations clear (*the weak view* of metaphor), but rather are powerful shapers of the very ways we think. Just consider how some of the other metaphors in the opening paragraphs shape our thinking: *basic* concepts, *units* in the course, *digging below the surface*, *deeper* meaning, and *impression*.

Notice the metaphors in the second conversation, which we purposely shaped around strongly contrasting views of the nature of the child and the task of the school. For Megan, the child's life and learning constitute a journey. Schools should watch and walk with them, helping when necessary. But Brian believes schools need to socialize children and prepare them to function productively in a nation's economic life. Our immediate concern here is not your view or our view of these understandings of the child and the school. Rather, we want to note how powerfully these metaphors work in educational language. *Accompanying children* and *equipping children* represent dramatically opposed educational metaphors, one quite humanistic and the other pragmatic and strongly oriented toward economic productivity. Clearly, these metaphors are not simply adornments meant to aid plain language in the job of making some educational concepts clear. Rather, these metaphors catch the essence or energy of two markedly different visions for children and schools. So, we ask, how important are metaphors in education? We take the position that metaphors are unavoidable, influential, and enriching. This book shows both how important they are and how they are important. Throughout, we will examine the metaphors that educators use to talk and think about a number of specific dimensions of education such as teaching and learning, assessment and spirituality.

Why ask about and consider the impact of metaphors? Teachers, principals and parents—in fact everyone, including students—think about students and schools using metaphoric language. But could we not get along just fine without metaphors? Could we not understand such important educational topics as teaching, learning, students, curriculum and assessment in non-figurative language? For decades philosophers and educational thinkers have debated the importance of metaphors in education (such as Black, 1944; Greene, 1971; Scheffler, 1971). One major writer on metaphor questioned whether metaphors are actually necessary and not just nice (Ortony, 1975, 1993). Despite the views of some that educators could manage just fine without metaphors (Miller, 1976), the authors of the chapters that follow believe that educational metaphors are not just nice, but that they powerfully affect teaching and learning, and, therefore, the lives of children and adolescents. Therefore educators need to evaluate how educational metaphors affect our praxis, and then choose carefully those metaphors within which we will locate our praxis.

Metaphors as Ornamental Language

Most of us likely first studied metaphors sometime in upper elementary school. We probably memorized definitions of *simile* and *metaphor,* some of us struggling to remember which one involved the words *like* or *as.* In their attempts to teach us about metaphor, our teachers may have quoted "My Love is Like a Red, Red Rose" from Robert Burns or the famous question in Shakespeare's Sonnet #18, "Shall I compare thee to a Summer's day?" Most of us likely emerged from secondary school with a generalized definition of metaphor roughly like that offered by Aristotle in his *Poetics* over twenty-three centuries ago: metaphor is the expression of one thing in terms of another (Aristotle, 1997). Aristotle's definition has much to commend it, most obviously that it is borne out by our experience. We all understand some difficult concepts—such as *valence* in chemistry, *supply and demand* in economics, the *ego* in psychology—better because someone used a metaphor to aid our understanding.

Years later, when a member of the Ski Patrol informs us that *avalanching snow is like wet cement,* we may show new respect for the posted boundaries on a mountain. Or when the Safety Branch of the Department of Transport tells us that *texting while driving is like drunk driving,* we may rethink our claim that we can both text and drive. Such everyday examples illustrate that, in some sense, both Aristotle and our English teachers understood something true about metaphor.

Metaphors may induce caution at ski resorts or on the road, but they may prove dangerous in other circumstances. A number of researchers have suggested in recent decades that metaphors operate at a much more fundamental level in cognition than we usually recognize. When we fail to notice their powerful role in thinking, we may go off in a dubious direction or make big mistakes. Rather than us using our metaphors positively at such times, they use us in unhelpful ways. Recall the conversations at the beginning of this chapter. What if teachers really should accompany children on a journey but schools see it as their primary mandate to prepare them for participation in a global economy? Or reverse the question. What if educators really should prepare children for economic participation but schools understand their primary mandate as accompanying students on their personal quest for learning? It is important which metaphors educators choose. Metaphors help shape the practices that educators follow. An educator working with a metaphor that does not reflect a school's mission and vision may well aim at goals that conflict with that school or its supporting community. Their students may well learn material and ask questions that are wide of the mark. We do not claim that a consideration of metaphors will answer all what schools are about. But, conversely, without thinking about the use of educational metaphors, we cannot fully understand what is happening in schools. So in this book we focus on this important question: How do the metaphors that we employ in education either deflect us from our proper work or move us closer to work that is proper, worthwhile and lasting? Related to this is the question of how the metaphors we use reflect our basic beliefs about schooling.

Metaphors as More Than Ornament

To explore whether metaphors actually function as more than linguistic ornaments, starting in the staff room as we did makes sense. We say this because it is in the staff rooms, among other places, that we will hear conversations among teachers. As we saw at the start of this introductory chapter, those conversations invariably include metaphors and, as such, reveal a great deal about how teachers think about their students and their work. Establishing whether metaphors function as something other than ornaments may require that we do some work outside the staff room, as well, perhaps in the linguistics, psychology or philosophy sections of the library. We say this because metaphors have become the subject of much academic dispute, with some claiming that metaphors function only as ornaments for anyone wanting to explain or express a difficult concept or idea, and others claiming that human cognition itself depends on metaphor. That is, the question of whether metaphors are necessary and not just nice just won't go away.

The contemporary debate about whether metaphors are "necessary and not just nice" began in earnest in 1980 with the publication of *Metaphors We Live By*, written by George Lakoff and Mark Johnson, the first of several books they have written about metaphors, cognition and society (Lakoff & Johnson, 1980). In this 1980 book, their most famous, they note that "most people think they can get along perfectly well without metaphor" (p. 3), a view which fits what we have been calling the ornamental view or the *metaphors are just nice* view. They point out that one reason people draw this conclusion may lie in the widespread perception that metaphor is basically a matter of language, not a matter of thought. In other words, if metaphors are ornamental, an individual speaker or writer has the choice of dressing up an explanation with figurative language or not. They continue,

> The concepts that govern our thought are not just matters of the intellect. They also govern our everyday functioning, down to the most mundane details. Our concepts structure what we perceive, how we get around the world, and how we relate to other people. Our conceptual system thus plays a central role in defining our everyday realities. If we are right in suggesting that our conceptual system is largely metaphorical, then the way we think, what we experience, and what we do every day is very much a matter of metaphor. (p. 3)

Lest any of their readers still wonder if Lakoff and Johnson have truly cast their lot with the strong view of metaphor, they end their opening chapter this way: ". . . metaphor is not just a matter of language, that is, of mere words. We shall argue that, on the contrary, human thought processes are largely metaphorical. This is what we mean when we say that the human conceptual system is metaphorically structured and defined" (p. 6). The passages we have quoted here make Lakoff and Johnson's view quite clear: metaphors are necessary.

They follow their opening assertions with a hundred pages of illustrations of how metaphorically we think and speak about the simplest, everyday matters. In Chapter 4 of *Metaphors We Live By*, for example, they give an extended treatment to orientation words such as *up* and *down*. In the fictional interchanges between teachers with which we began this chapter, one of our teachers voiced surprise that a student was experiencing difficulty in biology because she was at the top of the social studies class. We included that line intentionally to connect with Lakoff and Johnson's discussion. Educators frequently use words such as *top*, *bottom*, *up* and *down* to describe students, their performance and their grades (*performance* and *grades* are themselves metaphors).

As educators, we usually do not recognize words such as these as metaphors because they have been buried for so long in our cognitive framework that they are literally beyond notice. But we should notice them. We should notice how words like *top* and *bottom* contain a specific understanding of assessment, one based almost entirely on comparisons between students rather than on whether each student has achieved the objectives for the unit of study at hand. Lakoff and Johnson did not direct *Metaphors We Live By* at educators specifically, but they would applaud any educator who, as a result of reading their work, began to notice how powerfully metaphors shape our cognitive structure and thus how we view students and carry out our work as educators.

Understood this way, metaphors do not serve as mere accessories to thought; rather, they shape thought and serve as the condition of its very possibility. Lakoff and Johnson state that ". . . human *thought processes* are largely metaphorical" and that "metaphors as linguistic expressions are possible precisely because there are metaphors in a person's conceptual system" (p. 6, emphasis theirs). On this account, metaphor defines reality itself. Lakoff and Johnson argue boldly that any theory of meaning and truth ultimately rests on metaphorical understanding. In other words, we do not know directly but only through metaphor. As one might expect, Lakoff and Johnson have faced criticism for crediting metaphors with such powers.

If we reject Lakoff and Johnson's account, does the *metaphors are just nice* view remain our only remaining option? We believe not. We agree with the *nice* account inasmuch as different metaphors in fact do highlight and help educators notice features of teaching and learning that they might otherwise take for granted or miss altogether. But when we see the kind of persuasive and pervasive influence that various metaphors exert in school classrooms, staffrooms and offices, we know that we need more than the nice account offers. We want to acknowledge metaphor's influential role in how we understand teaching and learning, while at the same time withholding some of the power that Lakoff and Johnson ascribe to metaphor. In short, we desire space between. We will not call it middle ground because it may not be in the middle (and that metaphorical language would lead us astray in our thinking!). It may lie closer to the *nice* or the *necessary* end of the continuum, but we will not prejudge its place on that continuum by our choice of language.

We believe that educators need to organize curriculum, instruction, assessment, classrooms and schools using metaphors that they choose intentionally and deliberately. Metaphors do shape educational practice. If we do not choose our metaphors, our metaphors will simply choose us, quickly landing us back in Lakoff and Johnson territory. Having said that, we recognize the rationalism implicit in a claim that we choose our metaphors and that's that. Research shows that teachers change their metaphors over their careers, leading us to admit that not only do our metaphors shape our practices but our practices shape our metaphors (our thinking). Researchers Massengill, Mahlios, & Barry (2005) conclude from their studies that ". . . through the analysis of changes in one's own metaphor over time, changes in self-understanding can be identified and, where desirable, modified" (p. 214). Thus, as educators, our practices and our metaphors work in a dialogical relationship, informing and transforming each other over time.

Two questions remain for us to answer in this introduction: what aspects of educational thought do metaphors influence? How powerful are metaphors, really? We turn to the first questions regarding the range of influence of educational metaphors. We take it as commonplace that metaphors affect how teachers view and understand the child (Heath, 1999, and the "Metaphors for Learners" chapter in this volume) and that teachers' view of the child affects how they approach teaching and learning. Many researchers have discussed the ways in which metaphors shape how teachers understand teaching and the organizations in which they teach (Massengill et al., 2005). Other researchers and other authors in this volume have also examined metaphors for assessment, for curriculum, for spirituality and for many other aspects of education.

Many educators have noted the changes that pre-service and in-service teachers undergo when they begin to examine their own metaphors for teaching, learning and other aspects of education. Some researchers have explored how metaphors can give teachers a starting point to engage in self-reflection (Price, 2002) and can influence how they understand and engage in their own professional development (Caughlan, 2004). A group of researchers who followed secondary teachers from their final pre-service year through their first year as full-time teachers discovered a measurable difference between the metaphors the pre-service teachers hoped to teach by and what their practice actually looked like in their classrooms (Price & McGee, 2009). When teachers reflect on their own metaphors they may detect gaps between their thinking and their practice. For example, the teacher who sees her role both as police officer and gardener may see, upon reflection, that those two metaphors imply dramatically different visions of teachers and students—and that based on her evolving insights she begins to give preference to one even though she may still have occasion to use the other on certain occasions (Burkhalter, 1997; Woollard, 2004). Metaphors shape how teachers understand subject-area knowledge (Mahlios, Massengill-Shaw, & Barry, 2010; Ornstein, 1999), and how students learn that knowledge. Note the important part metaphors play in how we view this central question in contemporary education: do teachers transmit knowledge or do students construct knowledge? Our readers are familiar with the wording of the question, but many educators glide over its metaphoric character. Regardless of how one answers the question, it does illustrate the importance of metaphor throughout educational thought, discussion and practice.

The second question we noted was about the power of metaphors. Recall our caution regarding Lakoff and Johnson's strong thesis. We want to recognize that metaphors have power but we want to avoid any hint that our behavior is completely determined by our language and the models it implies. Still, we know that metaphors are not "just nice." Some researchers have concluded that metaphors shape teacher practice more powerfully than does a teacher's training (Noyes, 2006; Steele, 2003). However, it seems more likely that the metaphors that pre-service teachers adopt are modified or transformed through actual classroom experience. Another researcher has suggested that teachers can have their teaching practice frozen in time by metaphor. Curriculum, students, social conditions and society's needs all may change but some teachers carry on the same program year after year because they possess and teach out of a specific metaphor of teaching and learning; to use the language of construction, their thinking is *set*, like cement (Kercheval, 2006). Reworded to give some recognition to the strong view of metaphor, they carry on year to year as they do because a specific metaphor possesses them, often implicitly. In tennis language, it has *set* them.

Other research points to happier conclusions about teachers' metaphors. Some researchers have found that metaphors help pre-service and in-service teachers understand their own practice (Fenwick, 1996) or that metaphors help teachers critically examine and change their beliefs and practice as a result of what they find (Thompson & Campbell, 2003). One researcher concluded that metaphors have the capacity to lead teachers toward greater freedom in their understanding of instruction and curriculum, increasing their creativity (Efron & Joseph, 2001). Metaphors can help educators understand other educators' visions of teaching (Fenwick, 1996; Fischer & Kiefer, 2001). We have mentioned only a sample drawn from the thousands of studies of educational metaphors, and we have kept our summary of these various researchers' conclusions brief.

But we have recounted enough to make the point that while metaphors have the power to possess teachers, they can also be the means by which teachers gain new insights, new approaches to teaching and learning, and possibly even liberation.

The fact that we wrote this book shows that we believe that metaphors are powerful. But many have warned that metaphors have the power to mislead as well as the power to lead. It is certainly true that metaphors are limited. No single metaphor catches any teacher's entire vision or classroom praxis. Moreover, if pushed too far, metaphors may break down or give a skewed view. What is clear is that we need to consider teachers' metaphors in the overall context of their story and practice. (Smith, 2001).

The Chapters in This Book

In this chapter, two distinctions have emerged which we need to keep in mind throughout this book. The first distinction is that between what we have called the cognitive or strong view of metaphor and the ornamental, nice or weak few of metaphor (words we use somewhat interchangeably). The strong view has metaphor working deeply and invisibly in our thoughts and language, shaping how we see the world and how we act in day-to-day life, including classrooms. The weak view has metaphor as figurative adornment for literal language, a helpful add-on when one is blocked from finding the right way to explain an idea or concept.

We also need to note the distinction between uses of metaphors such as *top* and *struggle* that have actually become ordinary language (or what some linguists call *dead metaphors*) and the metaphors for schools, learners, teaching and learning, assessment and spirituality upon and within which educators shape their day-to-day thinking and practice. In this book we focus on the latter.

Each of the next eight chapters in this book explores metaphors for a specific aspect of education. The order of the chapters may not always seem sequential. That is because the questions they address—like schooling itself—form pieces of an interlocking jigsaw puzzle. As experienced educators well know, teaching, learning, curriculum and assessment are all inextricably intertwined, even though we need to regularly separate these aspects and component parts of education from each other for analysis. The next eight chapters in this book all focus on single puzzles.

In chapter 2, *Metaphors for Learners,* Carla Nelson and Ken Badley start by noting some of the connections between metaphors for teachers and metaphors for learners. From their past experience as classroom teachers and their current vantage point as teacher educators, they then trace the narrative roots of their own metaphors for learners, focusing on how they grew into the metaphors they now teach by. They also open up the question of consistency between metaphors and practice, asking how teachers can identify gaps between the two. In their view, such gaps serve as openings for new learning and movement toward consistency, movement they consider worth pursuing.

In chapter 3, *Metaphors for Teaching,* Tim Wineberg explores how metaphors for teachers shape their professional lives. He moves away from such common metaphors as the teacher as facilitator, artist, guide, and transmitter of knowledge. Instead, he probes the depth of the metaphors for teacher as servant, moral friend, mentor, covenanter, and moral companion. He develops the point that such metaphors must be both substantive and dynamic in order to be pedagogically compelling. After discussing both the potential impact and some of the limitations of these metaphors, Wineberg concludes that they are especially valuable for teachers of the Christian faith because classroom teaching and learning thus grounded will then nurture students to become morally responsive and responsible contributors to their culture. Wineberg consistently invites his readers to reflect on the focal practices by which they hope to make these metaphors real in their classrooms, and he notes that Christians especially have reason to recognize the moral imperative in these practices.

Educators use a variety of metaphors to describe the teaching/learning relationship, ranging from industrial metaphors in which schools are to produce a uniform product to agricultural metaphors in which teachers prepare and nurture young plants. Ken Badley and Jaliene Hollabaugh begin their chapter, *Metaphors for Teaching and Learning* (chapter 4), with transmission metaphors. In these metaphors, teachers become transmitters of knowledge and students become recipients. Next, they explore a cluster of facilitation, coaching, and guidance metaphors which tend to place teachers as people who support student learning from the side.

They conclude by examining catalyst metaphors in which teachers induce student learning by disturbing their students' peace.

Elaine Brouwer begins chapter 5, *Curriculum as a Journey Toward Wisdom*, by surveying five clusters of dominant curriculum metaphors. These include curriculum as a means of producing literate citizens, curriculum as a course for "getting there," curriculum as storytelling, and curriculum as a means of liberation. She ends her survey with a family of metaphors related to courtship, conversation, dance and encounter. She gives the lion's share of the chapter over to in-depth explorations of four specific metaphors, beginning with curriculum as a plan or path. She moves from there to curriculum as a process and then curriculum as a garden. She returns to the chapter title in her final section, examining curriculum as a journey toward wisdom.

Harro Van Brummelen's chapter, *Student Assessment: Hitting the Mark or Lighting the Candle* (chapter 6), first deals with the pitfalls of the two most common clusters of metaphors used for student assessment: assessment as measurement and assessment as inquiry. He shows that most teachers maintain an uneasy balance between these two. As an alternative, he suggests that if assessment is seen as a blessing, as grace, and as justice, it will change the common frameworks and practices of student assessment. Not only do those metaphors have the potential of forging better relationships between a teacher and her students, but they may also stimulate more successful learning in a more amenable and effective learning community context. He concludes by showing how the biblical notion of covenant can be an overarching metaphor for these three, one that avoids the reductionism of both assessment as measurement and as inquiry.

In *Princesses and Superheroes: Metaphors that Work Against Wholeness* (chapter 7), Alyson Jule explores how a consumerist society propagates cultural images and ideals for boys and girls that ultimately harm them. She notes how these mass media-shaped metaphors promote a vapid, emotionally stunted, and ultimately powerless lifestyle for both genders. She suggests that particularly primary teachers should use alternative and varied metaphors for femininity and masculinity, ones related to how humans have been created as *imago Dei*. This will involve, for instance, finding stories, movies, and fantasy play props that develop a fuller sense of self.

Two chapters specifically address matters of spirituality and faith. In *Metaphors for Spirituality in Public Educational Settings* (chapter 8), Monika Hilder begins with some of the pedagogical and ethical questions raised by educational policies that relegate religion to the private sphere. She synthesizes extensive research into fantasy literature, spirituality and ethics to suggest models of spirituality that would aid those seeking authentic modes of living in public contexts. Readers will take courage, for example, from her offerings of such ideas as "irrigating the imagination," "choosing mental furniture," "the invisible thread," and "breaching the wall." Hilder offers real substance for those students and teachers of faith whose vocation puts them in public school classrooms.

In chapter 9, *Metaphors and Models of Faith-Learning Integration*, Ken Badley reviews how various Christians have understood the popular phrase, *faith-learning integration*. He begins by surveying a cluster of five models of faith-learning integration that focus on knowledge and curriculum, concluding that such models come up short. Noting that some have understood integration to be more of personal and spiritual concern, he examines models that focus on the teacher's Christian character. Others have focused more on pedagogy and the moment-by-moment life of classrooms. Badley examines those models as well and then briefly looks at those institutional models that envision the whole school as the venue for faith-learning integration. He argues that the educator wanting to be thoroughly faith-full will find a model which attends to all three elements.

Conclusion

David Smith has described how we can relate the message of the Bible to education. He describes one such way as using and applying biblically-informed metaphors (Van Brummelen, 2009). True enough, looking at learners as image-bearers of God as Jule does is much richer than considering them as blank slates or as organisms to be conditioned. Similarly, some educators have developed metaphors of the teacher from the Bible: the teacher as steward, as priest, and as shepherd/guide. This volume demonstrates that metaphors from various sources can yield beneficial insights. What we do need to remember as we consider the metaphors by which we teach, is that those ought to be rooted in or at least in harmony with a worldview that shapes our way of life as well as our stance to education. We hope that you keep that in mind as you read the remainder of this book.

We believe educational metaphors are unavoidable, influential and enriching. We do not view the unavoidability as a negative. Rather, we see it as an opportunity for meta-cognition, an opportunity to think intentionally about how we think about education. In our view, there is no debate about the influence of metaphors, for good or ill. Having accepted that metaphors influence educational practice powerfully, we want to understand that influence and ensure that teachers and educational policy-makers direct it toward good ends. Ultimately, we believe that our educational metaphors can enrich educators' thinking and practice and thereby enrich student learning. The metaphors you teach by: can you justify them?

References

Aristotle. (1997). *Poetics* (G. Whalley, Trans.). Montreal: McGill-Queen's University Press.

Black, M. (1944). Discussion: Education as art and discipline. *Ethics, 54*(4), 290–294.

Burkhalter, S. B. (1997). *A study of metaphors in teachers' talk during and after a national writing project summer institute (inservice).* University of Texas, Austin, TX.

Caughlan, S. B. (2004). *High-school teachers' cultural models of English as a school subject.* Unpublished doctoral dissertation, University of Wisconsin, Madison, WI.

Dorn, S., & Johanningmeier, E. (1999). Dropping out and the military metaphor for schooling. *History of Education Quarterly, 39*(2), 193.

Efron, S., & Joseph, P. B. (2001). Reflections in a mirror: Metaphors of teachers and teaching. In P. B. Joseph & G. E. Burnaford (Eds.), *Images of schoolteachers in America* (pp. 75–91). Mahwah, NJ: Lawrence Erlbaum.

Fenwick, T. (1996). *Firestarters and outfitters: Metaphors of adult education.* Paper presented at the Canadian Society for the Study of Education, St. Catherine's ON. ERIC: ED400463.

Fischer, J., & Kiefer, A. (2001). Constructing and discovering images of your teaching. In P. B. Joseph & G. E. Burnaford (Eds.), *Images of schoolteachers in America* (pp. 93–114). Mahwah, NJ: Lawrence Erlbaum.

Greene, T. (1971). *The activities of teaching.* New York: McGraw Hill.

Greves, S. V. (2005). Butterflies in our classrooms: Using metaphors in teacher education. *The Teacher Educator, 41*(2), 95–109.

Heath, M. S. (1999). *Metaphors we teach by: Personal teaching metaphors and phases of teacher career development.* Unpublished doctoral dissertation, University of South Carolina, Columbia, SC.

Kercheval, A. (2006). *On the uses and abuses of the teacher-as-artist metaphor: The responsibilities of educating teachers as artists.* Unpublished doctoral dissertation, Indiana University, Bloomington, IN.

Lakoff, G., & Johnson, M. (1980). *Metaphors we live by*. Chicago, Illinois: University of Chicago Press.

Mahlios, M., Massengill-Shaw, D., & Barry, A. (2010). Making sense of teaching through metaphors: A review across three studies. *Teachers and Teaching: Theory and Practice, 16*(1), 49–71.

Massengill, D., Mahlios, M., & Barry, A. (2005). Metaphors and sense of teaching: How these constructs influence novice teachers. *Teaching Education, 16*(3), 213–229.

Miller, R. M. (1976). The dubious case for metaphors in educational writing. *Educational Theory, 26*, 174–181.

Noyes, A. (2006). Using metaphor in mathematics teacher preparation. *Teaching and Teacher Education, 22*, 898–909.

Ornstein, A. C. (1999). Analyzing and improving teaching. In H. C. Waxman & H. J. Walberg (Eds.), *New directions for teaching practice and research*. Berkeley, CA: McCutchan.

Ortony, A. (1975). Why metaphors are necessary and not just nice. *Educational Theory, 25*(1), 45–53.

Ortony, A. (Ed.). (1993). *Metaphor and thought* (2nd ed.). Melbourne: Cambridge University Press.

Price, C. G. (2002). *Exploring teaching metaphors: How they shape beliefs, professional knowledge and emergent practice of 1st through 5th year teachers*. Unpublished Dissertation, University of Louisville, Louisville, KY.

Price, C. G., & McGee, C. D. (2009). Reflecting on the use of metaphor: Two professors' processes of discovery. *The Teacher Educator, 44*(1), 56–69.

Scheffler, I. (1971). Educational metaphors. In M. Levit (Ed.), *Curriculum* (pp. 135–141). Urbana, IL: University of Illinois Press.

Smith, D. I. (2001). The Bible and education: Ways of constructing the relationship. *Themelios, 26*(2), 29–42.

Steele, U. D. (2003). *Generative leadership or generativity: Examining the potential of these metaphors for pedagogic praxis*. Unpublished doctoral dissertation, University of Calgary, Calgary, AB.

Stevens, D. E. (2006). *Of bricks and butterflies: Four teachers' quest for professional growth* University of Toronto, Toronto.

Thompson, L. K., & Campbell, M. R. (2003). Gods, guides and gardeners: Preservice music educators' personal teaching metaphors. *Bulletin of the Council for Research in Music Education, 158*, 43–54.

Van Brummelen, H. (2009). *Walking with God in the classroom* (2nd ed.). Colorado Springs, CO: Purposeful Design.

Woollard, W. J. (2004). *The role of metaphor in the teaching of computing: Towards a taxonomy of pedagogic content knowledge*. Unpublished dissertation, University of Southampton, Southampton, UK.

two

Metaphors for Learners

Ken Badley and Carla Nelson

A KINDERGARTEN TEACHER SMILES as she answers a question about the pupils that came to her classroom in the new school year, "They are a bunch of angels." Her answer might remind one of other answers teachers sometimes offer to the same question. "Little devils" seems to spring to more teachers' lips than one might wish. "Students—especially the youngest ones—are like sponges, soaking in everything a teacher says." "Students are like animals and they need to be controlled; their behavior needs to be shaped by means of a program of positive and negative reinforcement."

These four answers demonstrate some of the range of images and metaphors teachers use for students. In this chapter we will explore that range, showing as we do that the range is actually wider than these four examples. These examples and others like them illustrate how important metaphors for learners are to those who use them. At this point in the book, we do not need to argue the importance of the metaphors teachers have and use for all aspects of education, including learners.

From their study of educational psychology, most of our readers will recall the various *expectation effects* noted by researchers such as Rosenthal and Jacobsen (1968) and how those effects bear on the language we use for the students who walk into our rooms. The Pygmalion effect, as Rosenthal and Jacobsen described it in *Pygmalion in the Classroom*, refers to the way that language can shape teachers' expectations of students. The teachers among their participants who taught students who were "about to bloom" saw their students bloom. Those with students performing "below grade level" found that their students performed below grade level. In other words, Rosenthal and Jacobsen anticipated Lakoff and Johnson's *Metaphors We Live By* by nearly two decades. By doing so, they raised some very important questions for the teachers who use the metaphors we named in the first paragraph of this chapter and, in fact, for all teachers.

If we believe our new kindergarten classes to be populated by angels, will we see angelic behavior? If we call our middle-school students little devils—especially to their faces—will they act accordingly? In both cases, Rosenthal and Jacobsen would answer yes. While assuring us that our metaphors for learners heavily influence what happens in the classroom, they would also note they are not determinists about the Pygmalion effect. It is a general effect, one to which we will see exceptions. But on the whole, our metaphors will influence what we do and see. That influence recalls the double meaning in the title of this book: our metaphors allow us to see into our teaching and they also shape our teaching.

We have argued that our metaphors for students influence classrooms in important ways. In view of this importance, in this chapter we will explore in more detail the range of metaphors educators use for learners and the ways that those metaphors work. We will also examine the biographical sources of teachers' metaphors for learners and explore the question of alignment between one's metaphors and one's classroom practice.

The Range of Metaphors for Learners

In *Walking with God in the Classroom: Christian Approaches to Teaching and Learning* (2009), Harro Van Brummelen offers a comprehensive overview of the most common metaphors for teaching, those which are both biblically encouraged for Christian teachers directly and those which speak to all Christians and thereby indirectly influence the way we are to teach. As Van Brummelen points out, these metaphors all offer useful insights into teaching but none offers a complete understanding of the complexity of the teaching and learning process. Each of these metaphors for teachers implies a corollary metaphor for learners. Van Brummelen offers a catalogue of eight metaphors for teachers. They are:

- Teacher as *artist* evokes an understanding of learners as creative beings who approach content in original and inventive ways.

- Teacher as *technician* implies a view of learners as ones requiring structure so as to exert control and efficiency in the product to be learned.

- Teacher as *facilitator* presumes that learners will be successful learners when the optimum environment is offered.

- Teacher as *storyteller* implies that learners are characters in the story of content. Learning therefore requires learners to see themselves as contributing to the resolve of existing tensions and full participants in the unfolding story of our world.

- Teacher as *craftsperson* suggests that the skills and abilities the teacher possesses and continually develops through reflective practice directly influences learning. Learners therefore are at the mercy, so to speak, of the teacher's workmanship.

- Teacher as *steward* arises from the parable of the talents and encourages teachers to use their talents in service of the learners.

- Teacher as *priest* highlights the importance of the responsibility and calling of the teacher to foster a caring community in which learners encounter God's reconciling love.

- Teacher as *shepherd-guide* implies that learners are in need of direction—the guiding, structuring, unfolding, and enabling functions of the teacher as he or she encourages each learner to function fully as responsible and independent beings (Van Brummelen, 2009).

As we noted, for Van Brummelen, each metaphor for teachers implies a corollary metaphor for learners. In his view, learners have been viewed over the past three hundred years by educators in four primary ways.

For some educators, learners are conceived of as *receptacles of knowledge*—either as blank slates on which adults write knowledge or as piggy banks into which facts and concepts are deposited. Other educators hold the image of learners as *trainable objects* in need of structured behavioral sequencing of steps characterized by rewards and punishments. Still other educators view learners as *unfolding plants* who require the assistance of teachers to help them develop their natural, inherent abilities. Finally, some envisage learners primarily as *agents of social change*, a vision which necessitates that teachers offer opportunities for inquiry through which learners solve problems and think critically as they learn to take on their role of improving society.

Other educational philosophers make this discussion even simpler. They classify all metaphors for the teaching learning process into just two categories—received (or behaviorist) and constructivist (Cheng, Chan, Tang, & Cheng, 2009; Patchen & Crawford, 2011). Of the four categories summarized from Van Brummelen above, the first two—receptacles of knowledge and trainable objects—align most easily with the behaviorist orientation in that learners are on the receiving end of the teacher's initiative. The last two—unfolding plants and agents of social change—fit the constructivist framework most easily.

We say *most easily* in the last paragraph because, of course, the four categories Van Brummelen distinguishes do not mesh perfectly with the two-part framework offered by Cheng and her colleagues. Constructivism is itself metaphoric language and its meanings range across a continuum with a relatively conservative view on one end (in which students must make curricular knowledge their own) to a more radical end (in which autonomous students choose their own values without reference to any larger normative framework).

At this point, we do not need to decide between two, four, or any other number of kinds of metaphors for learners and we do not need Van Brummelen's four categories to mesh perfectly in a two-category schema. Still, we will return to these categories throughout the chapter as we explore the roots of our metaphors for learners and the ways that some of those metaphors work in actual practice.

The Roots of Our Metaphors for Learners

In our work as teacher educators, both of us have asked pre-service and in-service teachers to identify their metaphors for learners. We have heard a variety of such metaphors, ranging from the kite at the end of a learning string, the mailbox into which the teacher deposits letters of learning, and of course many of those that we repeated above from Van Brummelen's list. We keep asking teachers to answer this question—at whatever stage in their career—because we believe it helps them reflect on and understand their own practice.

Regardless of whether they tend toward received views of knowledge or constructivist views of knowledge, teachers' metaphors for learners raise some interesting questions: How is it teachers come to hold the particular images they do? Do teachers decide intentionally to adopt particular metaphors through a reflective and philosophical process or do they just grow into certain metaphors because of their experiences in classrooms? Do teachers intentionally shape their curriculum, instruction and assessment with a chosen metaphor in view and do they set about to create a classroom ethos consistent with their declared preference of one metaphor over another? How do educational ideals and educational experiences interact with and influence each other?

Crites (1971; 1979) reminds us that we don't just think up our story as we sit under a tree on a lazy afternoon. Rather, our stories evolve out of the very fabric of our biographies. Jean Gaumer (2000) focused her research on the influences of teachers' stories by asking pre-service teachers to recall what led them to adopt the metaphors they did. With these researchers, we believe that metaphors, like stories, emerge over time. Those teachers who were schooled in a context with an explicitly dominant worldview may have been told what image of learners they were to hold. Whether they subscribe to that party line is, of course, another matter. Most teachers develop their view of learners as one part of their view of people in general (what some call their anthropology), which in turn is part of their overall worldview. We develop and constantly adjust our worldviews as we live, with such major influences as our family and cultural background, our education, reading and exposure to other media, and positive and negative watershed events, whether unique to us or experienced by our whole society. Of course, many more factors than these help shape how we view the world; we have listed only a few major influences. But even our partial list helps give a context for the question of how we come to adopt or hold the images of learners that we do.

In the following section, both of us will tell some of how we came to the metaphors that we currently have for learners.

Carla's Story

My childhood included being part of a church community. Being part of my family meant worshipping, studying, and living alongside others who formed that community. My childhood also included schooling at the public schools in the neighborhoods and negotiating life with other children, including my siblings and some of the children my mother cared for as part of the day-home she operated. My report cards depict a learner with average achievement and average interest. I was a kid who would not dare to be in trouble with anyone—compliant, shy, and dutiful—an image that I know I expect to see evidenced from learners in my classrooms.

Being given direct responsibility for children through babysitting, nursery duty at church, and eventually taking on teaching-like roles in Sunday school and summer camps, my image of learners shifted. The children in my care were sometimes playmates and sometimes interruptions, likely depending on my mood, not on my developing worldview. Perhaps my mood still influences my image of the learners in my classroom.

As I entered post-secondary studies, not in education, learners were my livelihood. I taught music lessons as a part-time job to help pay university tuition. I remember looking forward to being with most of them, hoping they would have practised during the week, but I did not look forward to being with all of them every week. My job was to move these learners along as they explored a skill which their parents hoped they would acquire. Talent was not really part of the equation. Learners as a source of livelihood is an image I still hold to some degree.

A year of theological studies helped solidify the value God places, and therefore I place as well, on people, on learners of all ages. Becoming a teacher and a counsellor was the logical step for professional direction. I began to image learners as worthy of care and recipients of my help. Professional preparation meant learning enough so as to be effective and helpful. Those who would receive my expertise were in need. I was to fill the deficit. I affirmed the belief that all human beings need to be recipients of God's love, mercy, forgiveness and grace, and I regarded teachers who function out of the metaphor of learners as receivers are enacting God's ways with us.

My practice teaching took place in a comprehensive high school in a small town setting at which my supervising teacher had been teaching for years. He was known as a real character. His lessons were like stand-up comedy routines. When he wasn't "on," he would sit at the back of the classroom as the students worked on assignments, gladly engaging in learner-initiated conversations of direction and clarification. His learners were his audience, recipients of his talent. His goal was to have his learners perform well in their studies after being inspired by the performance he offered. His image of his learners was of budding stars, constructors of talents of their own after being receivers of his.

My image of those same learners was more practical, scientific even. They would influence my success. They were mitigating variables, each with the power to determine the outcome of this teaching experiment I was undertaking. They were infected cells to be controlled so as not to contaminate the direction of my lesson and my career. I am sure I must have given some thought to the potential damage I was doing to their school success. Because I can still recall several by name, I know I must have taken the time to get to know them as people held as precious by their parents, community and God. Certainly, I would have imagined what contribution each would make to the world after their formal schooling is completed. But, I don't remember doing so. I remember being concerned about what they would say about me as their student teacher.

The majority of the teenage learners in my first teaching assignment, English as a Second Language classes, had, within just weeks, arrived on the western Canadian landscape from worlds that bore no resemblance. The politics, the weather, the transportation, the food, and the school were all completely new for them. They were completely new for me. They wanted to be at school. They were eager to open books and hold pencils. They lined up to greet me, personally, with a bow at the beginning of the day as they also did at the school day's end to offer me their thanks. I was the first to receive their questions, the first to see their bewilderment, and the first to ask about their lives, past and present. Their lives—that's what they taught me—that's what they gave me. They were not just students: They were lives in the making. Preparing lessons, gathering the materials, and articulating assessment strategy were all framed with a purpose. Lives entered my classroom and my life. My image of myself as a person who teaches and learns, and of the learners as people who learn and teach, again shifted: learners became growing beings.

Colleagues in my doctoral studies held a constructivist image of learners, one that resonated well with my 'teacher-as-nurturer' image. Learners were seen by my research community as makers of their curriculum or as co-makers of curriculum alongside their teachers, even makers of meaning (Clandinin, 1986; Clandinin & Connelly, 1992; Clandinin et al., 2006; Huber, Murphy, & Clandinin, 2011). Classrooms, homes, and communities are all places, worlds actually, in which learners come to see themselves as knowers. Ideally, the more trust between the adults in these curriculum-making worlds, the less tension the learners will experience as they compose their identities as confident and secure knowers of themselves and their worlds. Teachers are to attend to their learners' diverse lives with humility, resisting arrogant perception, and, with loving playfulness, travel to the learners' worlds (Lugones, 1987, p. 8).

Several Kenyan teacher colleagues, while in Kenya, greeted me one morning by saying, "Very smart." To my North American ears, 'very smart" was a compliment to the presentation I had offered them the day before. It was a bit of a disappointment when I realized they were commenting on my outfit (smart meaning stylish) and not my intelligence. It made me wonder about the tendency I have to quantify the amount of cleverness learners possess. "He is not very smart," is often said either in a pitying way so as to reveal the belief that not much more can be expected of this student. Or, it is often said in a conclusive manner revealing the belief that this student is not deserving of much of my teacher energy. An amount is a quantity and, when I speak of 'smartness," am I presuming that students possess an unchanging, static ability that determines school success? There I go again, speaking inconsistently with my belief that learners are constantly developing.

I now find myself involved in teacher preparation. I marvel at the teacher candidates as they wrestle with the tensions they come to recognize between their beliefs and their practice. How, they wonder, can they believe that every learner is a precious gift from God while wanting to throttle a particular learner for disrupting their lesson? We both have admitted to feeling like frauds when confronted with the reality that our practice and our attitudes do not always align with the beliefs we hold.

Ken's Story

When I was young, my family read the King James Bible after dinner every night and I learned to read mainly by following along the very difficult English in that Bible. By the time I arrived at kindergarten at 5 years and 7 months of age, I could read quite well. My grade 1 teacher suggested that I move to grade 2, which I did in April of my grade 1 year. Other than enjoying social studies, I can't remember much of school from that point on. I did well academically through elementary school but lost my focus once in high school. From my perspective now, as a professional educator, I can see that I endured some truly bad teaching in high school. I followed my "B" average in grade 9 with a "C" average in grades 10 and 11. I finished my slide appropriately by failing Algebra and Literature in Grade 12, necessitating my attending night courses in an adult education program for the next year.

Despite having flunked out of high school—my description of it at the time—I never lost my love of reading. One day on the way home from work in downtown Regina (Saskatchewan), I stopped to browse in Canada Drug and Book and bought a copy of John Holt's 1967 book, *How Children Learn*. At the time, I missed the irony that someone who failed grade 12 was purchasing a school-reform book. Now, that irony strikes me with great force. At the time, I just wanted to see what Holt had to say and I had no understanding that school had failed me much more than I had failed school. Holt's description of classrooms as places of interest, fascination, and adventure resonated deeply with what I wished could have been my own experience. I now see that book as the beginning of my formation of a metaphor for learners as active agents in their own learning and as people deserving of respect, most of whom want to learn and will do so if presented with some question to pique their interest.

I could not have written the last sentence of the previous paragraph the day I finished reading Holt's book, but at the time I already had a nascent sense that the teachers at my high school largely neither recognized my abilities nor gave me anything to pique my interest. In fact, the vice-principal picked me out early as a trouble-maker and he treated me accordingly. He had that calculation exactly backwards and his attitude contributed to my four-year slide, anticipating Rosenthal and Jacobsen's conclusions about the effects of the language we use on the students we teach. I became a victim of the Pygmalion effect. From my vantage point today, I recognize that vice-principal as a man who had been overlooked too many times when he applied for principalships, and one whose negative image of students bore the fruit Rosenthal and Jacobsen predicted, in this case fruit that had effects reaching well beyond his office.

Also from today's vantage point, I see the failure of that high school to know me or to recognize my gifts as major factors in my developing another part of my image of learners. As I studied for my undergraduate degree in psychology and English, and then my after-degree B.Ed. in secondary English, I developed the conviction that because students are unique, teachers had to offer multiple kinds of assignments so that students could work in or at least closer to their areas of interest, passion, or ability. I'm not pretending here that I was Howard Gardner before his time, but simply that my own experiences in school—that is, my failure, my memory of failure, and my eventual understanding of the school's failure—shaped my emerging ideals for education and my metaphors for learners.

At some point in my higher education, I came across what many call catalyst metaphors of teaching and learning. In catalyst metaphors, the teacher's job is to stir the pot, disturb the student, force her to process what she is learning about so that she develops her own answer to the question in front of her. Teachers who operate with catalyst metaphors do not just give answers to students and tell them to copy those answers down. The strongest version of this metaphor may be teaching as burgling, implying that the teacher actually messes up the furniture in students' minds, forcing them to clean and rearrange. Educational philosopher, Maxine Greene, often said that the teachers' job was to keep the pain alive (a claim she also made for philosophy, Hostetler, 2005). My own response to several generations of students who complained that it hurt to have to think so hard was that, like real pearls, educational pearls result from irritation. In this educational metaphor, the teacher should irritate the student to induce learning. I would add that the teacher should do so in developmentally-appropriate ways; the teacher provides age- and ability-appropriate scaffolding for kindergarten pupils, doctoral students, and everyone between. The key here in our effort to understand metaphors for learners is that the learner will respond to the irritation by producing a pearl. I know that this effect, like the Pygmalion effect, is general; it does not always happen, but it happens most of the time.

For most of my teaching career, I have tried to understand a phrase that psychologist Carl Rogers first used before I began teaching. He said that teachers were to act as *co-learners* (Rogers, 1969) by which he did not mean that we don't know anything but rather that we need to be learning too, along with our students. In his wonderful book on epistemology for educators, *To Know as We are Known*, Parker Palmer (1983) offers his understanding of the relationship between student, teacher, and subject that is consistent with the idea of co-learners. Where the conventional understanding of teaching and learning is that the learners must, in a sense, go through the teacher to get to the subject, Palmer says that the teacher and students approach the subject together, both attempting to understand it. This joint approach to the subject implies humility for both student and teacher, but especially for the teacher. In my viewing myself as a co-learner with my students lies another component of my metaphor for learners, one for which I don't actually have a better label than that offered by Carl Rogers himsef: the teacher as co-learner.

Does my use of the phrase *co-learner* or my appreciation of Palmer's idea imply that I am a constructivist? Not at all. I believe the world exists outside of ourselves and our own minds. And I believe that teachers and students alike need to learn about that world. Unlike most of the teachers whose classes I sat in for my K–12 education, however, I also believe that students will be more interested in learning about the world outside themselves if they can see that their teachers are trying to understand the subject too, that their teachers don't think that they've arrived epistemologically. And to summarize my earlier points about my image of learners, they will be more inclined to learn about that world if their teachers can pique their interest, can present them with some question or problem which can't be solved in five seconds, and can help them find connections between their own experience and the curriculum materials.

Even as I write these words, my images for learners remain in development. They have been shaped by working with pre-service teachers and in-service teachers, and by teaching secondary students, undergraduates, graduates, and doctoral students in four Canadian provinces, two Kenyan provinces, and two American states. These varied experiences have shaped and continue to shape my metaphor(s) of the learner. I know that as long as I teach, I will continue to recalibrate my metaphors for learners. That recalibration must last as long as I teach because I genuinely wish to keep co-learning with my students (with all the adaptation that implies), and also because none of my metaphors for learners is sufficiently comprehensive to account for everything I have encountered and will encounter.

Realizing Our Metaphors in Practice

We have identified some main metaphors for learners and we have briefly recounted some of the biographical influences on our own images of learners. Now we wish to consider this important question: how do we, as teachers, realize (or make real) our metaphors for learners? In the words of Tim Wineberg (in this volume) what will be the focal practices by which we attempt to make real our metaphors in practice? Because we are imperfect humans, we know that we will not always realize our educational ideals or act consistently with our metaphors. However, knowing that we will not always succeed does not license us to quit trying. Parker Palmer says that part of the courage to teach is our willingness to identify our gaps and inconsistencies and to commit ourselves to work toward consistency and more truth as we carry out the teaching activities of instructing, assessing and reporting. He views this commitment and work as necessary if we are to move toward integrity and wholeness. The alternative, in his view, is fragmentation and death (Palmer, 1998).

Freese (2008) traced this movement toward consistency and wholeness with eight teacher candidates who participated in her research project. We find her work important for anyone wanting to answer the question about realizing our metaphors, and we find her participants' comments revealing and encouraging for imperfect educators like us. During the practice teaching part of their program, Freese's participants asked themselves the question: do I practice what I preach? The pre-service teachers in her study intentionally attended to the contradictions between the theories they held and their practice. For example, the four participants whose vocational goal was to teach science had all criticized the ways they had learned science (as students) as overly structured and inflexible. Yet, in their student teaching placements they found that they became "lecture driven" and "text centered" themselves (p. 69) Freese writes that her participants "mentioned how their undergraduate experiences were focused on content and facts, and how this transferred into how they taught. They acknowledged that they did not create learning environments which encouraged student inquiry" (p. 69). This discovery fits with a body of research suggesting that the ways teachers were taught themselves heavily influence how they will teach as teachers, despite what they learn in their teacher-training program (three such studies are reviewed in Mahlios, Massengill-Shaw, & Barry, 2010). The discovery also recalls the short list of metaphors for learners we included in the first section of this chapter. Notice the tension for Freese's teacher candidates between the images of students as receptacles for information and students as inquirers.

In her own reflection on her practice teaching, one of Freese's participants wrote about her struggle to develop teaching practices consistent with her beliefs.

> I wanted to raise students who would always try to grow from their mistakes and who know that they're not dumb if they make mistakes . . . it was a trait I wanted my students to have . . . I was afraid of making mistakes . . . I was scared to do and say something that might be stupid . . . My main stance in my teaching philosophy had been the idea of letting students make mistakes and to learn from them. Yet, this philosophy had been put in the back seat. (p. 69)

When this pre-service teacher uncovered the gap between her theory and her practice, she gave herself permission to make mistakes and thereby to make her mistakes a valuable part of learning. In responding to her mistakes as she did, she actually did what Westney recommends in an important book about music pedagogy, *The Perfect Wrong Note* (2003). In that book, he points out that in most circumstances students don't play the wrong note intentionally. The music teacher's task becomes to help students view their wrong notes as venues for learning and to guide students as they explore the reasons lying beneath their wrong notes. One of us (Ken, who does not teach music), uses this book in education courses because of its obvious application to most learning situations. Were Westney to sit down with the participant in Freese's study quoted above, he would approve of her approach. Through self-assessment, she saw the gap between her ideal and her practice and explored the roots of the inconsistency before trying to fix anything.

In our view, Freese used a practice that could benefit all teachers, both pre-service and in-service. When teachers reflect on and write about both their ideals and their practices, and then compare the two, they have occasions to see changes in their thinking. Teachers who engage in this practice also have opportunity to see the "uncovering and unraveling of their beliefs" and to "reframe their thinking about teaching" (p. 74). Freese's goal, and that of most teacher educators, is to help "preservice teachers sort through their conflicts and contradictions and examine their taken for granted assumptions, prior beliefs, and philosophies" (p. 74). To summarize Freese's work and our reason for including her in this chapter, we see reflection as the first step toward realization of one's metaphors and ideals in one's teaching practice. As we reflect on our practice, as we confront the gaps and consistencies, and as we examine the roots of those inconsistencies, we lay the foundation for moving toward consistency.

Conclusion

We began this chapter by noting how some of the common images of teachers link to the common metaphors for learners. For our purposes here, we thought it best to start with Van Brummelen's four categories of learner metaphors: receptacles of knowledge, trainable objects, unfolding plants, and agents of social change. Teachers adapt and change metaphors throughout their careers. They also blend metaphors as occasions demand. With some contents or on some occasions they may lean toward a received view of knowledge in which children are receptacles for the heritage that has been handed down to us. When working with some students or when approaching other learning materials, these same teachers may come to view their students more as unfolding plants. We do not recommend a single, best metaphor to our readers.

Having cautioned about searching for a single, best metaphor, we remind our readers that the Christian Scriptures describe humans as made in God's image. That metaphor applies to teachers and learners, and implies that we all are responsible, responsive and creative beings. As finite beings, we cannot comprehend or develop this metaphor fully in our lifetimes, as aspects of the richness of the whole teaching/learning relationship inasmuch as our calling as teachers constantly unfolds.

We recommend that you reflect on how your own biography has shaped your thinking about education generally and your images of learners in particular. Almost all of us have been students in school and have therefore had lots of occasions to think about how we would like to see it organized and about what ideals it ought to aim for. In this chapter, we used about 1300 words each to tell our stories. We encourage our readers to take several weeks to write, edit, and revise their own stories, attending to their metaphors for learners but also to the other metaphors dealt with throughout this book.

Having recounted your own teaching story and noted both your ideals for education and some of your specific metaphors, we recommend that you identify specific gaps or inconsistencies. Recalling Freese's pre-service teachers and Westney's concept of the perfect wrong note, we encourage exploring the roots and sources of the gaps rather than bemoaning the reality of imperfection. When teachers examine some of the possible roots of their inconsistencies they put themselves in a better position to address those inconsistencies.

Throughout this chapter, we have used the words *ideals, images,* and *metaphors* somewhat interchangeably. This was not careless usage. We believe that educators ultimately give expression to their deepest wishes—their educational ideals—in all the day to day interactions they have with the learners in their classrooms. Attending to these interactions and naming the metaphor at work in the moment is a way of coming to understand just how close we are to enacting those ideals with the learners in our care.

References

Cheng, M., Chan, K., Tang, S., & Cheng, A. (2009). Pre-service teacher education students' epistemological beliefs and their conceptions of teaching. *Teaching and Teacher Education, 25,* 319–327.

Clandinin, D. J. (1986). *Classroom practice: Teacher images in action.* Philadelphia: Falmer.

Clandinin, D. J., & Connelly, F. M. (1992). Teacher as curriculum maker. In P. W. Jackson (Ed.), *Handbook of research on curriculum* (pp. 363–401). New York: Macmillan.

Clandinin, D. J., Huber, J., Huber, M., Murphy, M. S., Murray Orr, A., Pearce, M., et al. (2006). *Composing diverse identities: Narrative inquiries into the interwoven lives of children and teachers.* New York: Routledge.

Crites, S. (1971). The narrative quality of experience. *Journal of the American Academy of Religion, 39*(3), 291–311.

Crites, S. (1979). The aesthetics of self-deception. *Soundings, 2,* 108–129.

Freese, A. R. (2008). Transformation through self-study: The voices of preservice teachers. In C. Kosnik, C. Beck, A. R. Freese & A. P. Samaras (Eds.), *Making a difference in teacher education through self-study: Studies of personal, professional and program renewal* (pp. 65–79). New York: Springer.

Gaumer, J. E. (2000). *Reflecting and reframing: Beginning teachers' use of metaphor.* Unpublished Dissertation, Columbia University, New York.

Hostetler, K. D. (2005). What is "good" educational research? *Educational Researcher, 34*(6), 16–21.

Huber, J., Murphy, M. S., & Clandinin, D. J. (2011). *Place of curriculum making: Narrative inquiries into children's lives in motion.* Bingley, UK: Emerald.

Lugones, M. (1987). Playfulness, 'world'-travelling and loving perception. *Hypatia, 2*(2), 3–19.

Mahlios, M., Massengill-Shaw, D., & Barry, A. (2010). Making sense of teaching through metaphors: A review across three studies. *Teachers and Teaching: Theory and Practice, 16*(1), 49–71.

Palmer, P. (1983). *To know as we are known: A spirituality of education.* San Francisco: Harper.

Palmer, P. (1998). *The courage to teach.* San Francisco: Jossey-Bass.

Patchen, T., & Crawford, T. (2011). From gardeners to tour guides: The epistemological struggle revealed in teacher-generated metaphors of teaching. *Journal of Teacher Education, 62*(3), 286–298.

Rogers, C. R. (1969). *Freedom to learn.* Columbus, OH: Merrill.

Rosenthal, R., & Jacobson, L. (1968). *Pygmalion in the classroom: Teacher expectation and pupils' intellectual development*. New York: Holt, Rinehart and Winston.

Van Brummelen, H. (2009). *Walking with God in the classroom: Christian approaches to teaching and learning* (2nd ed.). Colorado Springs, CO: Purposeful Design.

Westney, W. (2003). *The perfect wrong note*. Pompton Plains, NJ: Amadeus Press.

three

Metaphors for Teachers

Tim Wineberg

THIS CHAPTER EXPLORES THE importance of pedagogical metaphors in shaping the professional lives of educators. Over the years, a wide variety of such metaphors has been proposed to illuminate aspects of a teacher's identity. The most valuable ones are both universal and prototypical. They are universal because their enactment is normative at almost at all times and in almost all places. They are prototypical in that they serve as models for our own unique pedagogical stories. Moreover, because any one metaphor draws attention to certain aspects of pedagogical practice, but not to others, a *multiplicity* of images is required to capture the complexity of praxis.

Space does not permit a thorough survey of pedagogical metaphors in the literature on teaching. Before I describe five metaphors that I believe to be basic as well as deep, I will cite just a handful of others with a range in substance and suitability.

Educators have sometimes proposed metaphors not for their universal and prototypical value, but because of their personal appeal. For example, Kristine Johnson recounts some identities she assumed early in her career: teacher as *cultural critic, midwife,* and *resource* (Holberg & Taylor, 2006). Being already technically competent as a teacher, Johnson tried on these identities to get a better sense of who she was as a professional. Brian Hill (1976/2006), writing from a Christian perspective, applies the biblical concept of reconciliation to the educational context. Hill explores three aspects of teacher as *reconciler.* Teachers are called, first, to alert the child to the hostilities at work in society. They must also balance the affective and the rational dimensions of personhood and pedagogy. Third, they adjudicate the competing and conflicting interests at play in educational policy making. Shari Stenberg (2005) has offered the image of teacher as *hero*. On the other hand, John Parks (1999) rejects the heroic image and instead proposes three that evoke a sense of "carrying, containing, and preserving energy sources": *bag lady, Johnny Appleseed,* and *The Trickster.*

These authors do not offer highly detailed accounts of their metaphorical images. This may well be because their images do not represent a fundamentally vital aspect of pedagogy, or because they lack inherent depth of meaning. For example, *teacher as midwife* captures the sense of an educator's presence and support as students struggle to bring something new to life. However, the metaphor's potential to communicate more than this is limited. Similarly, *teacher as resource* suggests little more than the value of an educator's knowledge being shared. Its impersonal tenor also fails to convey the centrality of personal relationship in teaching and learning.

Better known metaphors include those of teacher as *stranger* and teacher as *artist*. Maxine Greene (1973) thoughtfully developed the first at some length. A number of scholars, including Herman Horne (1917), Dwayne Huebner (1963/1999) and Elliot Eisner (1998), have developed the image of teacher as artist. These two images have been fleshed out sufficiently for others to recognize their significance for pedagogy. Eisner, for example, highlights the artistry of educational *connoisseurship* and educational *criticism*. Other well-known metaphors are teaching as a moral craft (Tom, 1984) and teaching as storytelling (Egan, 1989). Teachers themselves use metaphorical images when they, for instance, state that rather than being a sage on the stage, they are a guide on the side. Usually the image of "guide" in this instance is used in the sense of being a facilitator of learning.

In reflecting on the potential of any metaphorical image, we need to examine which values and obligations the image presupposes. Does the image compel us to care for our students with more sensitivity and discernment? Does it direct us to where our concerns and duties ought to lie? Does it bring a greater overall coherence to our pedagogical understanding? Does it offer a standard that provides a corrective for inadequate or defective versions of practice? Does it enlarge our capacity for moral perception, imagination, and judgment? For a metaphor to be meaningful, it must recognize and enlighten the demands, difficulties, and delights of everyday pedagogical practice. Reflecting on pedagogical metaphors within this framework will gradually deepen and refine one's vision and images of practice. Wendell Berry expresses this understanding with eloquence: "If one's sight is clear and if one stays on and works well, one's love gradually responds to the place as it really is, and one's visions gradually image possibilities that are really in it. Vision, possibility, work, and life—*all* have changed by mutual correction" (1983, p. 70, italics in original). This is where pedagogical metaphors come in. Our moral sensibility and worldview perspective emerge gradually as our identity is shaped. Our identity, in turn, is shaped in large part by those images and their related narratives and worldviews in which we choose to dwell (e.g., Hauerwas, 2001). Therefore, one of our tasks as educators is to seek out pedagogical metaphors that are profound enough to shape our personal-professional identity.

This chapter explores five universal and prototypical metaphors for teachers: *servant*, *moral friend*, *mentor*, *covenanter*, and *moral companion* (from Wineberg, 2008). These images are *relational* images with sufficient depth and complexity to be ethically formative. They powerfully shape the way we envision ourselves and our obligations to students. When internalized, they mediate how we perceive, interpret, and respond to the ever-changing situations of practice. Each metaphor illuminates certain fundamental ethical aspects of pedagogical care. When thoughtfully appropriated, they provide clarity, order, and meaning to our perceptions and imperatives for our moral formation.

Teacher as Servant

"Teacher-servant" holds in tension both what a teacher is and is not. This metaphor uses the word servant to refer to something quite different from its normal use. This discord brings the word to life. It draws us in and sets our imagination to work in an effort to reach for new meaning. The other four pedagogical metaphors that follow should similarly stimulate acts of imagination and meaning-making, enabling us to see the work we do with fresh eyes.

At first glance, the image of servant may seem incompatible with the valued nature of pedagogical work. The role of the servant is marginal, without status, distinction, or influence. However, other dimensions of servanthood do shed light on the nature of pedagogy. First, servant-work is *necessary* work, vital for the life of the community. Also, servant-work is characteristically *attentive, unobtrusive,* and *gentle* or *un-self-assertive.* Moreover, servants are called upon to *set aside a measure of their self-interest.* The Bible prizes these three dimensions of servanthood where we find individuals like Moses and Jesus honored with the title of "servant of God."

So then, as the image of teacher-servant takes shape, what should fade is the image of passive individuals who dutifully follow directives in a menial task. What ought to emerge instead is the image of capable and esteemed public servants who optimally and creatively use the gifts embedded in their personhood. These are individuals who take the initiative to act, who discern and respond to real needs, and who selflessly serve interests larger than their own.

For a pedagogical metaphor to be compelling and morally formative, it must be substantive and dynamic. To this end, I explore each of my pedagogical metaphors in terms of *focal practices,* that is, intentional, regular, normative teaching activities (Borgmann, 2003). In this section, I highlight two focal practices of a teacher's servant identity. First, servant-teachers balance sacrifice with fulfillment. Second, they cultivate contemplative disciplines of self-detachment and receptive attentiveness.

Selfless service always requires a degree of discipline and sacrifice. What, then, is the nature of teacher-servants' disciplined sacrifice? What are some of its psychological hazards? And how does the practice of balancing sacrifice and fulfillment alleviate these hazards?

The men and women drawn to the teaching profession are typically helpful, caring persons. They are eager to play a part in the development of young people. Yet when these same individuals encounter intransigent conditions in schools, they often find the work wearisome and draining. Over time, this feeling can undermine one's passion and commitment to service. Many teachers come to experience a kind of hopelessness or cynicism about difficult students and their possibilities, or about altering the structural conditions of schools. This cynicism may lead to resentment and anger or to depression, despair, and ultimately an exit from the profession.

There are a number of other psychological hazards as well. For example, some teachers, innocently or through a misguided survival mechanism, may come to play dramatic, larger-than-life characters in their classrooms. And for some, what often begins as a ploy to gain recognition ends up developing into an inflated personality, a self which feels forever under-appreciated. Other practitioners may develop a sort of arrogance that comes from doing work that few people wish to do, or are capable of doing. Most teachers have at one time or another experienced something similar. Their teaching has provided an invigorating sense of meaning and identity. Yet these legitimate feelings have also given rise to illusions of self-importance. Whether subtle or extreme, the vanity born of self-sacrifice is always a distortion of servanthood.

In the life of dedicated practice the daily demands can be strenuous, but they need not be perilous to one's well-being. What is crucial here is a proper perspective on the nature of servant-work. Selfless service must never mean suppressing one's own self-development, or foreclosing one's legitimate needs and aspirations. The key here is balance. Self-sacrifice and self-fulfillment must dynamically balance each other if one's personal-professional life is to remain healthy and generative.

It is important here to recognize that the *level* of service and corresponding satisfaction are peculiar to an individual. Thus, what one teacher may regard as excessive effort, another may take in stride. Yet sacrifice and satisfaction may well operate in a healthy balance for each. In addition, the sacrifice-fulfillment equilibrium is *changeable over time*. After several years of practice, for instance, a teacher may become more fully attuned to her inherent work demands. She may become more sensitive to the contours of tasks and requirements, and more responsive to the particularities of persons and relationships. As she more fully devotes herself, she derives a deeper sense of teaching's internal rewards, thus more acceptably balancing sacrifice and fulfillment.

Furthermore, while the ideals of service are altruistic, we cannot dispense with honest self-scrutiny concerning our motives, desires, efforts, frustrations, and satisfactions. Balancing sacrifice and fulfillment always requires a measure of self-critique. Without critical self-understanding, we may deceive ourselves and compromise the ethical ideals of selfless service.

I now turn to a second focal practice, the discipline of contemplation. The discipline of contemplation can cultivate and strengthen the moral sensibility necessary for authentic servanthood. Contemplation delivers us from self-absorption. It directs our attention outward to our students, to our subject matter, and to the ideals of practice. This is what makes it a moral discipline. At root, contemplation involves a detachment from self that makes us attentive to others. This *self-detachment* and other-directed *attentiveness* are a prerequisite for a caring *responsiveness*. I will examine each of these disciplines in turn.

Self-detachment requires the sort of self-indifference that does not weaken our self-affirmation or self-esteem. Rather, it involves the practice of restraining our willful, self-centered tendencies. Self-detachment speaks of being gentle, humble, and reticent in our relationships with others. It aims to be vitally attentive without being obtrusively present. A contemplative self-detachment entails respect for human limits, a sensibility of when to draw back and when to stop, lest we interfere.

The discipline of self-detachment lays the groundwork for the discipline of attentiveness. Contemplation includes the setting aside of self-involved feeling and action in order to open up space for concentrated, receptive attention. Philip Jackson contends that attentiveness in teaching requires that we narrow and humble our vision: "The narrowing allows us to focus on features of the environment that we might ordinarily pass by—small details and minuscule events, happenings that come and go in a twinkling. The humbling, which goes hand in hand with the narrowing, turns us toward the ordinary and mundane and away from the dramatic and colorful" (1992, p. 84). Through years of studying classroom life, Jackson became convinced of teachers' need to strengthen their capacity to notice details and to probe beneath the commonplace for hidden insights and meaning. He also recognized that such fine-grained, discerning attention could only be cultivated from a sobering awareness of our ignorance. There is far more complexity before us in the classroom that escapes our attention than there is that we do notice and understand.

Unless our outlook is receptive and empathetic, our practice tends to be self-centered, resulting in impersonal and uncaring relationships. This is why self-detached attentiveness must always issue in caring *responsiveness*. Karl Barth emphasizes this link between attentiveness and responsiveness in his description of the service we owe in our vocations. We can achieve such service only by attending to details of persons and tasks with all the knowledge, capability, and devotion we can bring to bear. Barth writes, "the smallest things and simplest of relations and problems demand our acceptance of their particularity, our willingness to immerse ourselves in them. They certainly demand our devotion, and this may entail sacrifice . . . we are there to adjust ourselves to them in the measure and tempo and manner of our effort and movement, to take to ourselves their need and worth and purpose, and on these presuppositions to give them of our best" (1936/1961, p. 642). Of course, contemplative attention extends beyond an immersion in the particulars of our work. This is because the quality or character of such attention requires the cultivation of empathetic insight into the needs, values, and aims of persons and tasks. It is this quality of attention that enables us to respond in accord with such needs, values, and aims.

Teacher as Moral Friend

Most of us are not accustomed to thinking about the moral life in terms of friendship, or of friendship as being moral. Yet, genuine friends are moral friends. They are individuals who want the best for us. They are a force for good in our lives, actively seeking our well-being. Through their commitment and care, moral friends enable us to mature into the sort of people we could never otherwise have become on our own. Moral friendship, then, is a promising metaphorical image for educators and the work they do.

However, we can make a case for moral friendship in teaching at a more basic level. First, most would agree that the need to love and be loved is basic to the human condition. There is something inherent in our humanity, in our personhood, that can be realized only in and through a love of other persons. The assurance that others are *for us* is vital for stable, flourishing living. The natural condition of human life, then, is one of being mutually rooted in others.

Mutuality implies an obligation to love and care for others. If this is a fundamental reality of moral life, then we are obliged to respond to this call. Put differently, if our intention is for mutuality of love and care with every person we encounter, then friendships will tend to develop naturally in all of our personal relations, including those with our students.

The focal practice of fostering mutuality of love and care strengthens a teacher's identity as a moral friend. Two disciplines are basic to this practice. I explored each in turn here: the other-directed movement of recognition and response, and facility in the use of personal language. I then conclude with an examination of the essential components of moral friendship.

Philosophers such as Emmanuel Levinas and Enda McDonagh have sought to pinpoint what lies at the heart of every moral experience. They have perceived that we necessarily elicit a fundamental moral response whenever we stand before another person. Human presence demands our attention. It exerts a call on our lives. It demands *recognition* and *response*. The encounter is a moral one because we sense that we cannot be indifferent to another person's presence. Although there are degrees of possible response, not to respond is to choose to be immoral.

Recognition is the active acknowledgment that the other has a claim on our attention. We acknowledge particularity and uniqueness. We discern individual talents and gifts. We discover unique personalities and potentialities. But recognition also demands that we must recognize, appreciate, and honor their otherness.

To respond is to break out, even momentarily, from our world and enter the world of the other. In this other-directed movement, the self breaks free of its egocentrism. It becomes redefined as the other is made part of our world. There is a moral dynamic to responsiveness. We become part of a larger world than our own through care and love. In the process, we are freed from self-absorption and fearfulness.

This basic moral experience of being called out of ourselves and into relationship with another illuminates what it is to be a person. Personhood is a relational, communal concept. Relationships are not *external* to the self, but rather they are *constitutive* of the self. We must therefore recognize and respond to the call coming from the other. We must see it not as a threat or burden but as a gift or grace. Developed other-directedness is what characterizes moral friendship.

If recognition and response are fundamental to establishing and sustaining mutual relationships, so too is our use of personal language. In the learning environment teachers rely heavily on language that is *descriptive* and *directive*. This is understandable because we wish to inform with precision and clarity, and to get certain tasks accomplished. And yet, professional care requires that we see *personal* language as more basic to our humanity and our relationships (Peterson, 1989). Personal language uses words to express ourselves and to understand others. It acknowledges and celebrates the mystery of uniqueness. It expresses feelings such as anxiety, delight, appreciation, wonder, joy. It builds trust as care is offered and received. Through personal language, we enter into relationships and deepen them.

Yet personal language is often conspicuously absent when we are busy working in our classrooms. The unfortunate result is reducing human life to what can be explained or controlled. Because personal language sustains relations of mutuality, it must be primary in our exercise of professional care. "Primary" need not mean predominant. Yet it must regularly season our descriptive and directive language. While teachers have a great deal to teach and to accomplish, their primary role as moral friends is being present to students and nurturing their transformation. Therefore, we need to be alert to how descriptive and directive languages dominate our culture and institutions today. Our culture has conditioned us to use these sorts of language. Yet descriptive and directive languages disregard the deeply personal aspects of teaching and the place of the person who gives form and life to the role. Whenever we use descriptive and directive language, we stifle relationships and personal transformation. If we are to avoid an impoverished view of practice, we must become fluent in all three forms of language.

Earlier I mentioned that examining the components of moral friendship would shed light on the focal practice of sustaining mutual relationships. Unlike friendships based upon *pleasure* or *usefulness*, the discussion here centers on *virtuous* or *moral* friendship (Aristotle, ca. 330 BCE, 1158a). Such friendship is not constituted by a common purpose. Rather, moral friends are primarily interested in each other's well-being, not in what they can achieve in cooperation. John Macmurray claims that moral friendship is based on justice, respect for personal freedom, and treating each other as equals (1949, 1961/1999).

First, friendship is fundamentally a relation between equals, although this is not to suggest that only equals can be friends. Equality in moral friendship transcends differences of function, status, interests, gifts, or virtues. It rests on sharing each other's personhood. In this view, students have an equal moral status with teachers.

Second, personal freedom means that the relation is neither established nor sustained through force of will. As such, it allows for self-expression and self-revelation, freely given and freely received. A sense of security and acceptance in the relationship allows each person to be himself or herself, without having "to play the part."

At times though, through imposing our own willfulness in the class-room, we fail to honor fully students' equal personhood. We constrain their freedom to be co-inquirers with us. Teachers must always try to see students as joint participants in the moral life. They must recognize that friendship with them is moral if it intends to preserve their free-dom and equality as moral agents. This means, for example, that together with students we develop a humble and receptive spirit that enables us to enter into the conversation and actions initiated by each other. In this way, teachers grant students the dignity of becoming willingly involved in teacher-initiated actions. Teachers, in turn, engage in genuine dialogue with students.

How does justice, the third constitutive principle of friendship, fit into this picture? The focus so far has been two persons in isolation from all other relationships. Yet if a friendship excludes others, then its motive is a negative one. If two friends defend against intrusion, it would un-dermine the relationship itself. In a genuine friendship, two friends will welcome others into their circle, to welcome community. Justice, then, serves to safeguard this inclusivity or equality of relation.

Teacher as Mentor

Mentors typically take on a variety of roles, such as motivator, tutor, role model, and sponsor. As important as these roles are, it is not the function-al aspect of mentorship that this section highlights, but the *gift of self* that is involved. The gift of one's interest, joy, knowledge, and understanding is what ultimately enriches and brings something to life in another per-son, even in the grade-school context. Since mentorship is a gift between persons, an appropriate place to begin is with a consideration of the focal practice of gift-giving.

A gift naturally possesses the power to delight us, to move us, to revive our souls. We never acquire gifts through our own efforts, will-power, or purchasing power, nor can we demand them or barter for them. Others bestow them on us. Once bestowed, the spirit of a gift retains its power and vitality, often long after being given, through the memories of generosity that lie behind it.

Regular rituals and traditions of gift-exchange tend to characterize the life of small closely-knit groups, such as families or clans. By contrast, in our market economy exchanges between persons are typically self-interested, instrumental, and impersonal. They lack the emotion and personal relation of gift exchange, and the enduring fulfillment that results. Yet because gift exchange *does* satisfy deep needs, there will always be a motive for relationships to move beyond the merely transactional. And when gifts circulate more widely than an exchange between two friends, communal bonds of gratitude and fidelity become established. This circulation gives coherence and stability to moral communities.

The gift of self that mentors offer serves as a catalyst for transformation in others. Gifts that possess the power to transform us touch us at a deep level. The acceptance of the gift results in a new, fuller identity. However, we cannot appropriate a gift until we meet it on its own terms. This requires that we become adequate to the sacrifice and labor of the gift, that we become sufficiently empowered to hold it. Lewis Hyde (1979) traces out the phases that accompany the sharing of a transformative gift such as mentorship: the gift is given, received, appropriated over time, and ultimately passed along to others. All this is done in a spirit of gratitude.

These phases deserve a fuller consideration in the pedagogical context. A mentor establishes a relationship with a protégé. She initiates the gift exchange by awakening or stirring the learner. What must then follow is the generative, identity-shaping phase of laboring. The learner must feel and embrace the proffered future. Receiving the gift as a true transformational possession may require many years. The labor is not so much dutiful obligation as it is a responsive effort in gratitude for the gift given. It is an inventive labor that reflects the desire to achieve, to become, and so to fulfill these possibilities affirmed by the teacher-mentor.

It is only when the gift has done its work in us, only when diligent labor has transformed us, that we can then pass it along to others. Bestowing the gift on others, which was once given to us, brings to completion the labor of gratitude, and confirms the genuine acceptance of the original gift. Students often feel a debt of gratitude for past teachers, even though they have forgotten the particulars of what they learned. Often they remember the *person* of the teacher—their joyful enthusiasm, self-discipline, and dedication.

A second focal practice of a teacher's identity as mentor overlaps with gift-giving. It is the discipline of cultivating pedagogical virtues and relations. Pedagogy denotes more than instruction. It grounds instruction is in a deep understanding of the learner, as well as in an engagement of the learner's intentions, interests, and desires (Fenstermacher, 1990, p. 137). Pedagogy presumes that teachers possess a relational knowledge of young people. They understand not only how they might think or view the world, but also their inner life and uniqueness as persons.

Many practitioners take a narrow view of professional care. They fail to grasp the full scope of pedagogical responsibilities that accompanies their role as *in loco parentis*, literally "in place of parents." This legal responsibility obliges teachers to protect and nurture young people. They must craft an educative environment that sustains their sense of wonder and possibility in the world. Such responsibilities demand a number of corresponding moral qualities, including *self-expenditure* and *compassion*. William May (2000) judges that these two qualities are vital, given the imbalance in knowledge and power that exists in the pedagogical relationship. Self-expenditure defines the teacher primarily as giver. However, teachers do not give in the same way benefactors or philanthropists do—out of their surplus. Rather, they receive a portion of their identity from the relation itself through their self-sacrifice. Compassion is related to self-expenditure for it literally means to "suffer with." When compassion marks the pedagogical relation, teachers suffer with students by identifying deeply with their fears, their frustrations, and their urgencies. Teachers learn and display compassion through their nuanced knowledge of students—their capacities and possibilities as well as their difficulties, anxieties, and vulnerabilities.

Educator Paulo Freire (1998) highlights a number of other virtue-like qualities that emerge out of the demands of the teaching practice: "a generous loving heart, respect for others, tolerance, humility, joyfulness . . . perseverance . . . hope, and openness to justice" (p. 108). Max van Manen adds, ". . . a sense of vocation, a love of and caring for children, a deep sense of responsibility, moral intuitiveness, self-critical openness, thoughtful maturity, sensitivity toward the child's subjectivity, an interpretive intelligence, a pedagogical understanding of the child's experiences and needs, improvisational resoluteness in dealing with young people, a passion for knowing and learning the mysteries of the world, the moral fibre to stand up for something, a certain understanding of the world, active hope in the face of prevailing crises, and, not the least, humor and vitality (1996, p. 46). Such qualities must be fixed in our character if students are to sense that they are the genuine motives of our actions.

Note that other authors have developed the metaphor of guide or the biblical notion of shepherd. These metaphors overlap a great deal with the image of mentor described above, especially with respect to the discipline of cultivating pedagogical relations. One focal practice emphasized by the metaphor of guide is that teachers help students discover knowledge. On the other hand, the image of mentorship does more to highlight the gift of self. This once again shows that a combination of images enriches our pedagogical insights (for a discussion of the teacher as guide see, for instance, Van Brummelen, 2009).

Teacher as Convenanter

This section sets the focal practice of gift-giving in mentoring relations within the wider framework of covenantal relationships. Here I highlight just two focal practices that sustain a teacher's identity as a covenanter: acknowledging mutual gift, need, and indebtedness; and offering the gift of hospitality. I begin, though, with a brief examination of the nature of covenants.

Covenants and contracts both specify certain duties or obligations. But a critical difference exists between the two. A contract stipulates the conditions of a short-term alliance between persons to satisfy mutual interests. By contrast, a covenant unites persons with shared values in a long-term commitment to the good of a community. Covenants presuppose communal bonds, an enduring fidelity to the other's well-being, and an assumption of obligations to others which can be personally transformative.

Covenants and covenantal relations have a rich history. Covenant is a central feature of the Hippocratic Oath, dating from classical times. Covenant was also central to the life of ancient Israel: covenants of friendship, the covenant of marriage, covenants between nations, covenantal duties to sojourners in the land, and of course, their primary covenant with God. Four basic elements comprise a covenant in the biblical tradition. First, an original *gift* is extended between potential covenant partners. Second, a *commitment* or *promise* is made out of a grateful responsiveness to this gift. Third, covenant partners demonstrate a *fidelity* to their commitments that shapes their life together. Finally, there is a periodic *ritual enactment* to commemorate the covenant (May, 2000). It is one's responsiveness to a gift that in a profound way characterizes a covenant. Fidelity to one's commitments always emerges out of a sense of indebtedness and a sense of grateful response to a gift.

Covenant-making expresses something universal in human experience. That is because the making and keeping of promises deepens one's character and sense of identity. Edward Langerak (1994) highlights three implications of covenantal arrangements. First, gift-giving takes place in a context of openness and trust. The partners are therefore to some degree vulnerable to each other. Second, a covenant cuts deeper than a contract because it involves a promissory event that touches one's identity, and that shapes one's future life personally and communally. Third, a covenant calls for a fidelity that ranges beyond the known particulars of a contract, to unforeseen and unforeseeable possibilities.

A number of focal practices can assist us in strengthening the covenantal nature of our pedagogical relationships. First of all, we need to remind ourselves of the context of *mutual need, gift,* and *indebtedness* in which we undertake our work. We must always view the professional relationship as reciprocal in nature, rather than one-sided. William May (2000) points out that acts of giving and receiving—acts of care and generosity on the one hand, and gratitude and obligation on the other—serve to nourish pedagogical relationships: "Students need a teacher, but the teacher also needs students. They provide the teacher with a regular occasion and forum in which to work out what he or she has to say and to rediscover the subjects afresh through the discipline of sharing it with others" (May, p. 123).

Need, gift, and indebtedness extend beyond the day-to-day professional relationship. This is because every professional incurs a substantial *prior indebtedness* to the community—to their own teachers, to earlier generations of and current educators, and to the wider society for the privilege of practice and financial rewards. Importantly, then, a covenant serves to correct the misconception of some teachers that their work is a *gratuitous* rather than a *responsive* act.

Another focal practice that serves to strengthen covenantal bonds with our students is the exercise of hospitality. In a sense, young people are strangers in our midst, not yet part of the community in that they do not share in a set of common understandings and experiences. To be hospitable is to open a space for sharing common meanings and jointly constructing ways of being together in community. Through the *gift* of hospitality, its underlying *commitment*, and the *fidelity* that it demonstrates and evokes, we invite young people into the life of a covenant community and its traditions.

We can express the concentrated and thoughtful work of extending hospitality and fashioning welcoming spaces in many ways in the classroom. All of us feel welcomed and cared for when our needs are anticipated and recognized. Conversely, care imposed on us by another's idea of our needs disempowers us. Therefore, the work of gracefully extending hospitality must involve the experience of students themselves.

Henri Nouwen (1980) calls attention to two basic movements in extending hospitality: *revealing* and *affirming*. Students have been in the receiving mode to such an extent that many can hardly imagine that they have something valuable to offer, something to *reveal* to others. Therefore, as receptive hosts, teachers have to remove these misconceptions. They have to help students see that their experiences, their insights and beliefs, their intuitions, feelings, and hopes are worthy of serious attention. This underscores the importance of drawing out an articulate consciousness in students, through having the narrative capacity enter into that individual's life story. It demands the sort of pedagogical sensibilities we explored in earlier sections: self-detachment, attentiveness, and receptivity; recognition and responsiveness; and the gift of self.

What is revealed as good and worthwhile needs to be *affirmed*. As encouraging hosts, we must not only bring hidden talents into view, but we also help students to strengthen these talents and to move on with renewed self-confidence. In addition, we have a covenantal obligation to develop within students their capacity for discerning what is true, and worthy, and life-bearing. Our task, then, is to affirm young people for what they are becoming, and help them distinguish between what is good and what is less worthy in their lives. Affirmation can take a variety of forms—a smile of approval or understanding, a word of encouragement, a gesture of delight or thankfulness. It even extends to pedagogical purposes: affirming students' innate desires and interests, their creative impulse and capacity, and their efforts in knowledge-making. Whatever form our affirmation takes, students come to see through our acts that they are not deficient and ignorant. Rather, they are guests in the classroom community who belong. They have a contribution to make, and they have a story to tell.

Teacher as Moral Companion

Hope is an act of imagination. When hope is directed to the good of others, it is an act of moral imagination. As students' moral companions, teachers embody hope. The metaphor of companion implies a kind of gracious reciprocity in the relationship. Two features of this image deserve highlighting: the closeness of shared effort and responsibility, as well as the hopefulness of being on a journey together. Closeness and hopefulness, when understood as disciplines, can both be pursued as focal practices.

Closeness allows for perceiving the needs of others and accommodating oneself to their idiosyncrasies. Close companionship involves a sensitive sharing which assists in the other's journey of self, without imposing or being intrusive. The aim is to enable self-determination through a caring relationship that strengthens others' capacity to understand themselves and their aspirations. Moreover, closeness speaks of "being with" others and persevering together through difficulties. This element is so easily lost when interactions between teachers and students are predominantly task-oriented.

A companion is literally one who shares the same bread. The sharing of a common meal is an enduring picture of acceptance, hospitality, and intimacy. Moreover, a deeper understanding of shared bread is that of shared resources or shared gifts in general. Moral companionship, then, speaks of a willingness to share with others the necessities of life. When teachers and students come to view each other as moral companions, they recognize that they are involved in an adventure in which each has the privilege and obligation of offering support to the other. The resources they bring, and the time and talents they offer—all serve to bring them closer together.

Hopefulness, the other quality of good companions, conveys a confidence and insight into how the journey together can be accomplished and the inner transformation that attends it. David Hansen writes:

> This sense of hope, metaphorically speaking, helps the teacher rise each morning to face another day of educational uncertainty, adventure, challenge, difficulty, and accomplishment. This sense of hope helps the teacher move into the unpredictable pedagogical world rather than remain on the sidelines—as do educators who have lost their passion for educating and who end each school

day the same way they began it, with their sensibilities and commitments unchanged by their time spent with children or youth. In contrast, for teachers who retain their hopefulness, and who appreciate critically the significance of the work, it is almost impossible not to be affected and moved by students. (2004, p. 131)

Hope has to do with the human condition, with the difficulties and possibilities of communities and their members. In his work on hope, however, Farley (1996) notes that hope can be ambiguous, because its meaning depends upon whether it is understood subjectively or objectively. In its subjective meaning, hope denotes a personal disposition, narrowing it to one's own inner confidence. It is then just an extension of one's efforts. On the other hand, hope can refer to an objective future—what is to be, without personal involvement. Either perspective alone is inadequate. But to simply paste subjective and objective dimensions together does not in itself give a corrective. It merely identifies the hoped-for object with an individual's wishes or desires.

A further problem is that individualistic hope is vulnerable to ups and downs. Such hope wavers as confidence in oneself or in the believed-in object waxes or wanes. Although hope inevitably has a specific, concrete component, authentic hopefulness is more a way of being than a way of believing. It is a patiently persistent, courageous, active waiting grounded in the life of moral companions journeying with us.

In offering professional care, this hopeful way of being in the world communicates to our students that they are not journeying alone. Through our own posture of hopefulness they come to embrace their future expectantly yet soberly. Thus, hope ought to be understood as a value and ethos at work in the character and traditions of a community. Hopeful communities have past traditions, ways of keeping mutuality alive, but they are also oriented toward the future. Even when circumstances are difficult, such communities have positive, expectant ways of being together. Individuals, then, do not typically invent references of hope. Rather, they uncover them in the memories, symbols, traditions, and institutions of their communities—even their school communities. Pedagogical hope is always an active, expectant concern for the life and growth of students entrusted to our care.

Hope, when understood as an active, persistent, patient waiting, contains tension. It implies both waiting and action. Waiting is inescapable. This is because hope is situated precisely where conditions are difficult. There is struggle, frustration, and suffering because there is an absence, a need. So in hope we wait, we yearn for what has not yet arrived. Yet hope does not wait in a passive, resigned, or indifferent mood. It is dynamic and expectant: wide-awake, engaged, intense, and interested. To hope is to wait persistently, with robust determination. Such hope is a way of living toward the future—and the future of our students—with courageous imagination. It understands that external circumstances or events do not completely determine any of our lives. Yet it does not exist in wishing or naïve optimism. Instead, it is an attitude of heart and mind that transcends the logic of predictions and probabilities. It persists largely by drawing on traditions of hope and resistance across time, and the company of hopeful companions in the present.

Conclusion

In conclusion, I want to locate this topic in the broader context of faith, and, particularly, Christian faith. Such contextualization is appropriate because it is faith that gives us our identity and our basic attitudes toward God, humankind, and all created realities. Christians understand the life of faith as an ongoing response of love and gratitude to a gracious, loving God. They believe and understand that life's meaning, value, and direction all find their source in Jesus Christ. And as they grow in the life of faith, they find that every aspect of their lives—their interests, desires, feelings, and understandings—becomes increasingly oriented to Christ. They come to experience a greater freedom from powers that dominate and enslave them, and a corresponding freedom for the things of this world that, they believe, God entrusts to them.

Educators are entrusted with a high calling. Education is a helping profession that seeks to meet a fundamental human need, the need for knowledge. This qualifies it as a moral activity since it requires vulnerable persons to trust in the knowledge and skills of someone who professes to care for them. Teachers professing a religious faith will exercise their professional care in accord with their faith that impels them "to see everyone with whom we have any contact at all as our neighbor, to be respected, loved, helped, and served according to what need he or she has and what power we have to assist" (Packer, 1996, p. 15).

This concept of enacting neighbor-love in the exercise of professional care enables us to understand our life and our professional life as integral or whole. And if the life of faith is a morally coherent one, then personal and professional spheres merge in a way of life that draws upon the depths of our personhood. In this view, we should not view professional knowledge and skills in isolation from our broader intellectual and moral capacities, our emotions, and the various qualities of our character that have shaped our faith.

This chapter has focused on five metaphorical images that should hold particular currency for persons of faith. As such, they inform how our moral sensibility affects our pedagogical practices. Moral sensibility is a term that encompasses our capacities of moral perception, intuition, imagination, courage, and judgment. These capacities are crucial in teaching, because they enable sensitivity and skill in dealing with students and with the ever-changing situations of practice. The metaphors of teacher as servant, as moral friend, as mentor, as covenanter, and as moral companion, while not all-encompassing, will help us to contemplate, develop, and apply our moral sensibility so that our students may, in turn, become morally responsive and responsible contributors to our world.

References

Aristotle (1962). *Nicomachean ethics* (M. Ostwald, trans.). (1962). Indianapolis, IN: Bobbs-Merrill. (Original work published c. 330 BC)

Barth, K. (1961). *Church dogmatics: Volume III. The doctrine of creation: Part 4.* G. W. Bromiley, & T. F. Torrance (Eds.). Edinburgh: T & T Clark. (Original volumes published 1936)

Berry, W. (1983). *Standing by words.* San Francisco, CA: North Point Press.

Borgmann, A. (2003). *Power failure: Christianity in the culture of technology.* Grand Rapids, MI: Brazos Press.

Egan, K, (1986). *Teaching as storytelling: An alternative approach to teaching and curriculum in the elementary school.* London, ON: Althouse Press.

Eisner, E. (1998). *The enlightened eye: Qualitative inquiry and the enhancement of educational practice.* Upper Saddle River, NJ: Prentice-Hall.

Farley, E. (1996). *Deep symbols: Their postmodern effacement and reclamation.* Harrisburg, PA: Trinity Press International.

Fenstermacher, G. (1990). Some moral considerations on teaching as a profession. In John I. Goodland, Roger Soder, & Kenneth A. Sirotnik (Eds.) *The moral dimensions of teaching* (pp. 130–151). San Francisco, CA: Jossey-Bass.

Freire, P. (1998). *Pedagogy of freedom: Ethics, democracy, and civic courage.* New York: Rowman & Littlefield Publishers.

Greene, M. (1973). *Teacher as stranger: Educational philosophy for the modern age.* Belmont, CA: Wadsworth.

Hansen, D. (2004). A poetics of teaching. *Educational Theory, 54*(2), 119–142.

Hauerwas, S. (2001). *The Hauerwas reader*. John Berkman & Michael Cartwright (Eds.). Durham, NC: Duke University Press.

Hill, B. V. (2006). Teaching as reconciliation. *Journal of Education and Christian Belief, 10*(1), 33–41.

Holberg, J. L. & Taylor, M. (2006). The teaching self. *Pedagogy: Critical Approaches to Teaching Literature, Language, Composition, and Culture, 6*(1), 1–6.

Horne, H. (1917). *The teacher as artist*. Boston: Houghton-Mifflin.

Huebner, D. (1999). The art of teaching. In *The lure of the transcendent: Collected essays* (pp. 23–35). Mahweh, NJ: Lawrence Erlbaum.

Hyde, L. (1979). *The gift: Imagination and the erotic life of property*. New York: Vintage Books.

Jackson, P. (1992). *Untaught lessons*. New York: Teachers College Press.

Langerak, E. (1994). Duties to others and covenantal ethics. In Courtney W. Campbell (Ed.), *Duties to others* (pp. 91–108). Dordrecht, Netherlands: Kluwer.

Macmurray, J. (1949). *Conditions of freedom*. London: Faber and Faber Ltd.

Macmurray, J. (1999). *Persons in relation*. New York: Humanity Books.

May, W. (2000). *The physician's covenant: Images of the healer in medical ethics*. Louisville, KY: Westminster John Knox.

Nouwen, H. J. M. (1980). *Reaching out: Three movements of the spiritual life*. London: Collins.

Packer, J. I. (1996). Faith, covenant, and medical practice. In E. C. Hui (Ed.) *Christian character, virtue, and bioethics* (pp. 11–24). Vancouver, BC: Regent College.

Parks, J. G. (1996). The teacher as bag lady. *College Teaching, 44*(4), 132–137.

Peterson, E. (1989). *The contemplative pastor: Returning to the art of spiritual direction*. Grand Rapids, MI: Eerdmans.

Stenberg, S. (2005). *Professing and pedagogy: Learning the teaching of English*. Urbana, IL: National Council of Teachers of English.

Tom, A. (1984). *Teaching as a moral craft*. New York: Longman.

Van Brummelen, H. (2009). *Walking with God in the classroom: Christian approaches to teaching and learning*. Colorado Springs, CO: Purposeful Design Publications.

van Manen, M. (1996). Fit for teaching. In William Hare & John P. Portelli (Eds.) *Philosophy of education: Introductory readings* (2nd ed.) (pp. 29-51). Calgary, AB: Detselig.

Wineberg, T. (2008). *Professional care and vocation: Cultivating ethical sensibilities in teaching*. Rotterdam, Netherlands: Sense Publishers.

four

Metaphors for Teaching and Learning

Ken Badley and Jaliene Hollabaugh

WHEN TALKING TO TEACHERS, students, or members of the public, you will hear people use a wide range of metaphors about education. Other chapters in this book focus on metaphors for teachers and learners, curriculum, assessment, and other aspects of schools and education. In this chapter we examine metaphors for the relationship between teaching and learning, arguably the key relationship in schools. Notice our language already. What if we had said that teaching/learning is the key *exchange* in education? The word exchange would already prejudge how teaching and learning connect as concepts. The term relationship does the same. We point this out to remind all of us of Lakoff and Johnson's argument (1980) about the importance of metaphor in our thinking. We have a hard time finding language devoid of metaphors to describe what takes place in education. So we ask, what kind of relationship do the two central activities of teaching and learning have to each other?

Many people have explored this question. Their answers, which range from hunches to research-based conclusions to worldview-based declarations, fill the education shelves in post-secondary libraries. We begin our exploration here with a survey of a few metaphors for the teaching/learning relationship, demonstrating their great variety. We will then examine three key metaphors in detail. There are, of course, many more, but for others we point you to academic library databases.

The three clusters of metaphors we explore in major sections in this chapter are transmission, facilitation, and catalyst metaphors. The dominant class of metaphors for teaching and learning focuses on the transmission of information. Many educators also use the language of facilitation, guidance, and coaching to catch what transpires in teaching and learning. Here students set out to accomplish certain learning goals with teachers providing assistance. Finally, the catalyst metaphor suggests that the student learns best when facing cognitive dissonance, and where the teacher's job is to create that dissonance. Before treating those three clusters of images in more depth, we survey a few other metaphors for teaching and learning.

Some educators use medical and psychological metaphors. These range from dentistry (Fischer & Kiefer, 2001) to psychotherapy (Efron & Joseph, 2001). Generally, such metaphors portray teachers positively, as people who meet the needs of their students. However, Ivan Illich, a radical critic of schooling, used a medical metaphor negatively to argue for what he called deschooling (Illich, 1970, 1977). He wanted to remove teaching and learning from the institutions which, in his view, had monopolized it and defined it for their own purposes of social control. In Illich's metaphor, teachers are like doctors and teaching is like the practice of medicine. Students come to teachers for healing of what ails them—and what ails them is ignorance. Using this metaphor and a few similar ones, Illich built a rather detailed critique of schooling as part of his larger utopian vision for education and all of society. We disagree with Illich. We believe that ignorance exists independently of institutional solutions used by schools to treat it. On the other hand, we applaud Illich for calling as early as 1970—decades before the internet—for people to use computers to connect learners with those who could teach them what they wanted to know. The medical metaphor, whether used positively or negatively, illustrates the power of metaphors. For instance, Illich's s metaphor may plant seeds of doubt about whether schools really do solve the problem of ignorance.

Historically, many educators have used military and agricultural metaphors to describe teaching and learning. Military metaphors generally project messages of toughness, conformity, and uniformity. This last aim—uniformity—was shared by the many educators (mainly in another era) for whom schools served as factories whose purpose was to produce uniform and productive people. In agricultural metaphors, students grow and teachers nurture. Besides these common metaphors, there also are a growing number of educators who view the school classroom as a place of respite where people find hospitality, a biblical virtue (Anderson, 2011; Bennett, 2003; McAvoy, 1998).

The range of metaphors from which educators choose indicates something about the important role of metaphors in our thinking about education. This broad range also shows that metaphors for teaching and learning are somewhat tangled up with metaphors for teachers, metaphors for learners, metaphors for curriculum, and so on. You should keep that in mind as you read this chapter on metaphors for teaching and learning.

Transmission Metaphors for Teaching and Learning

Transmission is arguably the oldest and most recognizable metaphor for teaching and learning. The word *transmission* dates back to the early 1600s and connotes movement from one thing or being to another thing or being. For example, each society possesses its own stock of knowledge, and teachers, according to transmission metaphors, have the responsibility to pass part of that stock of knowledge on to the next generation. For many educators, the metaphor of transmission epitomizes the transactions involved in teaching and learning. All knowledge must come from somewhere, and when knowledge is shared by one person with another, the goal is generally for the other person to internalize that knowledge. Teachers have the professional responsibility to prepare for, lead in, and communicate knowledge from themselves to their students.

Transmission metaphors connect to an old educational debate about the Latin origins of the word education. Some point to the Latin word *educare*, which means to raise a child or animal, as etymological evidence that children are like clay which teachers shape. A quite different metaphor has children as growing plants in need of a gardener, a picture that fits better with the Latin term, *educere*, which means to lead forth, draw out or elicit (Scheffler, 1964; Zachariah, 1985). These contrasting possibilities illuminate the historical tension in defining the relationship between teachers and learners. The definition of education and the metaphors for teaching and learning consciously or unconsciously used in classrooms have an impact on what transpires and on how students perceive themselves as learners.

For example, picture the arrangement of desks in a classroom approximately one-hundred years ago. In this picture the straight rows of desks are quite likely screwed to the classroom floor. This desk arrangement implies that the business of the classroom is for one person to transmit important information to a group of people. In other words, arranging desks for transmission reflects the Latin term educare (to train a child or animal). To use the most common language of a century ago, teachers were to *teach* pupils. Notice the etymological connection between the pupil in a classroom and the pupil in your eye; the function of both is to admit light. Also, notice the word teach that we italicized just above. A century ago, teach did not imply facilitating table groups, organizing jigsaws, telling students to engage in a quick think-pair-share, or directing students to fill out exit slips. Teaching meant telling, transmitting. Many educational terms flow from and support that metaphor, such as ideas come across, teachers try to get through to students, or teachers deliver content which students absorb. To this day, if you watch children playing "school" you will likely see the older one standing and instructing the younger one(s), a reason to believe that transmission may remain for many the default metaphor of teaching and learning.

Perhaps it is not surprising that transmission metaphors now carry strong negative connotations for some students and educators (for example, Reinsmith, 1992). At the surface level, transmission metaphors may imply that teachers simply relay information to students, a task that some today might argue can be done more effectively and at less cost by computers, tablets, or smart phones. True, lectures and rote memorization can be boring at times. However, both are essential for some forms of learning. For example, try getting by without knowing the alphabet, part of that unglamorous yet necessary foundation for other learning and for life itself. We are the first to admit that some teachers who function only in the transmission mode—especially if they understand transmission to involve mainly themselves talking—do it poorly and need to expand their repertoire of teaching strategies. Yet we challenge the view that developments in computer and phone technology imply that we can dispense with teachers. Also, we want to point to the many vibrant and engaging teachers who use transmission of knowledge effectively. Arguments that transmission of knowledge is passé or necessarily inferior pedagogically is simplistic.

One characterization of poor teaching often unfairly associated with transmission metaphors has teachers cramming vast gobs of information into students' brains in short and limited blocks of time, usually through lecture. Teachers and professors who adopt transmission metaphors may rightly think that their responsibilities include passing knowledge to students. But such metaphors do not offer a license for bad teaching. A common question often debated in discussions of transmission metaphors is whether the regurgitation of information demonstrates learning. At times, the regurgitation of information does demonstrate learning. We believe that transmission metaphors accurately represent what teachers should be able to do in their classrooms: have knowledge to transmit. However, there are boundaries to the transmission metaphor that, when crossed, reek of teacher ignorance at best and arrogance at worst—and fail in that students do not attain the stated or implied learning outcomes.

Unreflective teachers who work under the umbrella of transmission metaphors may consistently overlook the experiences, cultural differences, language barriers, and prior knowledge that students bring to the classroom. Arrogant teachers may think too highly of themselves and their own knowledge, coming to believe that they are the only light by which pupils learn. No teacher, no matter how bright, knows everything. The arrogant teachers we describe here implicitly demean students. Such teachers' interpretations and views both grow from and nurture a loss of appreciation for their human imperfections, for recorded history's imperfections, and for their students' rightful place as agents in their own learning.

When a teacher attempts to become the sole transmitter and interpreter of knowledge (the *principal source and cause* of learning) within a classroom, meaningful learning is easily undermined. For instance, the perspectives and conclusions of students are devalued, and such transmission may also be used to promote and justify indoctrination. In the view of St. Thomas Aquinas, God is the only principal cause of learning, not the teacher or the student. Thomas' claim contains insight regarding any teacher's role as a transmitter of knowledge. Even those who question Thomas' claim will recognize that both the physical and social worlds are so complex that even an interdisciplinary genius such as Leonardo da Vinci lacked the capacity for complete understanding. Furthermore, we all depend on communal knowledge developed and deemed trustworthy over a period of time. So we conclude that teachers need to seek the path of humility. We work within paradigms that, as Thomas Kuhn (1970) pointed out, may well be flawed. They deal with issues where we struggle with apparently irresolvable paradoxes. Their interpretations of

phenomena are often ones that compete with a spectrum of alternate interpretations. If we believe, as St. Paul put it, that "now we see only a poor
reflection" (1 Cor 13:12), then teaching and learning need to suggest awe,
wonder, and even uncertainty about God's world. The writings of both
Thomas Aquinas and Thomas Kuhn suggest humility. And throughout
Scripture, we are reminded that whatever we as teachers and students
accomplish together we accomplish only by God's grace.

Facilitation, Guidance, and Coaching Metaphors for Teaching and Learning

Course evaluation forms often include a statement such as "The teacher
[or professor] facilitates student learning well." If you think for a moment
where we use the word *facilitator* in other contexts—a conference or
meeting facilitator, for example—you quickly recognize the salient premise of the facilitation metaphor: learning comes primarily from within
students but teachers seek to put in place optimal conditions for learning.
As did transmission metaphors, facilitation metaphors imply roles and
activities for both teachers and students.

Founded on this premise, Montessori classrooms are set up to encourage student learning by promoting an environment where students
direct their own learning through exercising some freedom to choose
what, when, and how they want to learn. Note the phrase *some freedom*;
in Montessori classrooms, teachers do guide. For students who are already self-motivated, who recognize their inherent abilities to discover
and create and who realize that they are the primary source of their learning, this view of teaching and learning can work well. We know that not
all students meet the conditions we just named. We have observed, as
have all teachers, that students who have a difficult time remaining self-
directed need teachers who do much more than facilitate. Or, perhaps
facilitation metaphors need to imply a greater degree of teacher-direction
than many people often infer. We view teachers who guide well as those
whose clear expectations and explicit directions create a structured and
productive learning environment. It is difficult even for the most motivated learners to remain focused and engaged on the educational tasks at
hand all the time. A good facilitator actively prepares for the distractions
that will inevitably occur in any learning environment.

Generally, teachers working within a facilitation metaphor see themselves as people who help their students discover knowledge, solutions, or processes on their own. They see themselves as "guides on the side." Facilitators create the opportunities for students to learn. To aid understanding of facilitation in teaching contexts, however, we might recommend substituting the metaphorical synonym *prime mover* for the word *facilitator*. Prime mover language more openly recognizes the teacher's dual roles of preparing the environment for student learning to occur and guiding the process as it unfolds. In addition, prime mover language counters a false and rather commonplace opposition between transmission metaphors and guidance metaphors. It would be nearly impossible, for example, for teachers to prepare for student learning to occur—whether working under transmission or guide metaphors—without some expert knowledge in the area which the students were to study. Hence, guidance metaphors must necessarily include space for aspects of transmission, and prime mover language better describes this necessary partnership.

One educator (McKenzie, 1998) has developed a list of verbs to describe teachers who act as guides: circulating, moderating, validating, redirecting, trouble-shooting, observing, assessing, encouraging, modeling, questioning, challenging, motivating, and even disciplining. To the degree that McKenzie's (1998) list is right, teaching as facilitating or guiding entails much more than simply allowing students to discover and learn on their own. Facilitating also involves constant assessment and re-calibration in order to provide each learner with the support they need to complete the educational tasks in front of them. When we view facilitating learning as a highly active process, we see that guidance and coaching metaphors belong in the same discussion as facilitation metaphors. Also, when we view facilitation as more active, we also may partially solve the problem of those learners who don't meet the three conditions we listed regarding Montessori schools.

It was not by mistake or oversight that we combined the facilitation and guidance metaphors in the preceding paragraphs. We recognize that some educational theorists keep them separated, in part because in our ordinary speech we recognize that the facilitator might not need as much knowledge on a given subject matter as a guide (Efron & Joseph, 2001; Rogers, 1969). For example, a guide shows us the highlights of a place and perhaps warns us about pitfalls and places to avoid. Guides often do the driving, using their local knowledge of shortcuts, traffic patterns, and prices. Guides help travelers understand the relationship between the map and the actual territory. Many mountaineers know that without the help of guides, they would not get to the top at all. A facilitator, on the other hand, is not always expected to have the same degree of intimate knowledge on a subject. One can facilitate a large corporate business convention, for example, without the knowledge required to lead the breakout sessions. We want to combine both images and we believe that classrooms are best served by teachers who have the skills to serve as an active facilitator as well as the expert knowledge usually expected of a guide. One writer, in fact, has offered an understanding of the Latin root of the word education that we did not mention in the discussion of transmission metaphors above, an interpretation that seems to combine the roles of facilitator and guide. Rechtschaffen (2011) argues that the word education originates in the Latin *ex duco*, which means both from within and to guide. Especially in educational contexts, the metaphors of facilitation and guidance really should be together within the same discussion, in part because teachers should be expected to do both.

In facilitation metaphors, the teacher's role is to create opportunities for the student to learn. The guide's role is to possess knowledge of what the students need to learn. Coaching metaphors, however, encompass both facilitating and guiding, while adding a very important condition: the ability to motivate. Good coaches are able to inspire those they coach to perform at their highest level, whether in training, in competition, or in life experiences. In the classroom, the ability to motivate learners to perform at their highest level is especially important when teachers operate within facilitation or guidance metaphors. Teachers who view students as the primary source of their own learning will need to provide the external encouragement their students need to move toward their learning goals.

Coaching metaphors rightfully bring the thinking and methods of respected coaches into the academic realm that any teacher—coach or not—can use (more discussion of coaching metaphors appears in Austin, 2000). Successful coaches try to prepare their athletes both mentally and physically for competition. In a classroom, that competition could take the form of a test, an invention, a skill, or the acquisition and application of new knowledge. In the training of athletes, coaches allot time for both repeated practice of key skills and for the incremental development of new skills, while providing motivation and encouragement. However, the most powerful contribution of coaching metaphors may be the focus they place on students as participants in their own success. Athletic coaches may be talented, but individual athletes shoulder the primary responsibility for their performance.

Just as facilitation and guiding metaphors did, coaching metaphors involve both teachers and students as participants in the learning process. If someone told us that the teacher in the room we were about to visit worked within a coaching metaphor, we would enter that room expecting to see the teacher work within certain patterns consistent with the metaphor, as described earlier (e.g., an emphasis on practice, preparation, and encouragement). But we ask what we would expect to see if students were working within a coaching metaphor? Graves (2006) offers some examples of what we might see and suggests that several benefits accrue when students are able to embrace a coaching metaphor.

> The most valuable component of having students think of a teacher as a coach is how they are forced to rethink their role in their performance. Sports is an arena still relatively unburdened by society's pervasive culture of blame. In defeat, coaches often take the blame, but players rarely permit them, repeating sports clichés like "Coach put us in a position to make plays, but we didn't make the plays and we lost." After a win, the players repeat, "We needed to step up and make plays, and we did that this time." Moreover, coaches are never blamed for the difficulty of the opposing team, and indeed players relish playing tough opponents. The sports attitude discourages the unexamined assignment of credit and blame often overheard in hallways after an exam (Graves, 2006, paragraph 8).

If Graves is right, and we think he is, then coaching metaphors imply that students must take significant responsibility for their own learning. This is not a simple case of doing the math; teachers remain responsible for a thousand details related to the learning that is intended to happen in their rooms. Still, coaching metaphors can clearly bring an educational advantage to any classroom if they help students grasp their own responsibilities for learning.

Perhaps we take an unconventional route when we cluster the commonly recognized metaphors of facilitation, guiding, and coaching within the same family. We do so because we believe that each of the three metaphors overlaps the other two to such a high degree that they are hard to pry apart. In a Venn diagram representing these three metaphors, the cross-hatched area would dominate the diagram. However, we want to point out some cautions and boundaries with these metaphors. If teachers working within facilitation, guidance, and coach metaphors stand too far to the side (speaking metaphorically), some students may never discover the rich resources of historical knowledge that they might discover in a classroom constructed around the idea of transmission. The potential for such gaps in student learning demonstrates why we have argued that this cluster of metaphors must include space for transmission and why teachers must have knowledge to transmit. Left to their own devices, some students will explore only what interests them, not what is in their interests. These metaphors, understood and applied correctly, do not get teachers off the hook for directing students to that which is in their interests to learn.

We raise another caution related to this cluster of metaphors: students who have not been initiated into the idea that they are the primary instigator of their own learning may resist or flounder in this model of instruction. Perhaps rightly so (given the usual expectations society and students have for schools), such students will wait for their teachers to give them the information they need. One researcher, who explored the language of teacher-centered and student-centered classrooms, concluded that many teachers try too hard to get out of the way of student learning (Santoro Gomez, 2005, 2006). Teachers must strive to find the balance that all students need (and most desire) between teacher-direction and self-direction. We know that the point of balance differs for each student, depending on various factors, including raw ability. Thus teachers need to build flexibility into their instruction and assessment plans so that students who struggle to get onto their educational feet can walk, while others are freed to fly. Effective teachers find the delicate balance between the time available for teaching and learning and the energy required to learn new knowledge thoroughly. Teachers who adopt facilitation, guidance, or coaching metaphors uncritically may create a classroom where student learning progresses too slowly due to a lack of purposeful planning, instruction, and encouragement. In recent decades, many teacher educators have focused unduly on facilitation, guidance, and coaching models as if transmission were never needed. Unfortunately for the preservice teachers who graduate from some programs, facilitation is simply not enough. Transmission, when executed in the form of single-mode, day-after-day, boring, direct instruction, may have earned a bad reputation for transmission metaphors. This is unfortunate because in the end, facilitation metaphors may not be sufficient in themselves. It turns out that highly effective teachers work in both kinds of metaphors and mix their instruction.

Catalyst Metaphors for Teaching and Learning

For some teachers, catalyst metaphors best catch the feature of teaching that leads most effectively to student learning: student engagement. In catalyst metaphors teachers stir students in their thinking—stir the pot, so to speak—perhaps by playing the devil's advocates on some points of controversy (Efron & Joseph, 2001), or by disturbing students in some other way. Some educators, noting Socrates' unrelenting use of questions, claim that he worked in a catalyst metaphor. The phrase *Socratic teaching* has connotations of lively to and fro between teachers and students. In the words of one educator, catalyst teachers start fires (Fenwick, 1996).

We call on another metaphor to illustrate this one. Whether natural or cultured, pearls result when the oyster coats a grain of sand with enzymes. In catalyst metaphors, teachers are to insert pedagogical grains of sand and thereby irritate their students' thinking. Thus irritated, the students will coat the pedagogical irritants and ultimately produce educational pearls, so to speak. Teachers in this role consciously weave hard-to-answer questions into the course materials and instructional plans. A junior-high textbook project in which one of us was involved included questions at three different levels of difficulty. The easiest questions appeared under the heading Checkpoints and the moderately difficult questions were labeled Reflections or Activities. But the most difficult and demanding questions always appeared under the heading Brain Freeze. The point of these questions was that textbooks, which often fail to challenge all students in a given class, owe the brightest students questions capable of giving them a good (if metaphoric) headache. Interestingly, the editor had not previously heard of a brain freeze and accepted the usage only after her nephew confirmed that it was real language.

Teachers wanting to justify catalyst metaphors will point to such benefits as higher student engagement with the learning materials at hand and thereby greater enjoyment of school overall. They may note that catalyst metaphors make teaching more interesting for teachers as well. Admittedly, the Socratic method is not for everyone, and catalyst metaphors have an intuitive appeal to educators more inclined to risk and adventure. But anyone who would work with a catalyst metaphor in view needs to hear one disclaimer and recognize several constraints.

The disclaimer is simple. Highly engaging classes, whether underwritten by catalyst metaphors or by some other metaphors, do not necessarily lead to appropriate learning. Debating a contentious law, current event, or social policy, for example, may get the full attention of all the students in a classroom but meet none of the curricular objectives for the course. In the language of sufficient and necessary conditions, engagement might be necessary (or at least desirable) for appropriate learning to occur, but it is not sufficient.

First, teachers who habitually ask difficult, non-factual questions may be excellent at generating student engagement. However, such teachers must also learn to listen carefully to students' answers for appropriate learning to occur. Such listening allows teachers to engage students with the necessary secondary questions that check for understanding and push for clarification. Such listening also allows teachers to explore what students think might be some of the implications of their initial answers. Catalyst teaching thereby involves allowing—or sometimes forcing—students to see where their own ideas lead. Frequently, such freedom results in the expression of views contrary to what teachers might want expressed, requiring significant teacher self-confidence as well as confidence in the students, in the learning process and in God's Spirit. Besides all these forms of confidence, teachers who would build a portion of their program on catalyst metaphors will need exceptional classroom leadership and discussion-leading skills, as well as a commitment not to manipulate instruction toward their own desired conclusions (which students usually spot in a second anyway).

For students, seeing where their ideas lead is not always comfortable, and catalyst metaphors therefore imply two additional conditions for teachers. First, in catalyst teaching, teachers must recognize a boundary: how much pushing is appropriate for students, given their intellectual and emotional maturity at any given age? This is especially true when we recognize that most secondary students and almost all students younger than them have difficulty seeing the shades of gray in questions that, contrary to what they might prefer, simply have no right or wrong answer. Connected to this first condition of age-appropriate pushing, catalyst teachers (like all teachers) must provide an atmosphere of safety. A prerequisite to honest and sometimes blunt conversation is that those in the teaching-learning space function as a community of trust, to use Parker Palmer's language in *The Courage to Teach* (1998). Teachers who prefer catalyst metaphors must ensure that their students experience the learning/teaching space as safe. Students are willing to face hard challenges to their thinking if they believe they are in a safe place. But when students feel threatened, they will not be open to the new learning that their teacher may intend, a claim borne out by recent developments in neurology and especially research focused on the part of the brain known as the amygdala, which plays an important role in our responses to fear and anxiety (Cozolino, 2002). In short, once students learn that a room is unsafe they have trouble learning that it can be safe. Thankfully, the corollary of that statement is also true, reason enough to focus on building the community of trust that Palmer talks about before trying to create a Socratic academy.

We cannot simply breeze by the importance of safety in catalyst metaphors of teaching and learning. Researchers in the last couple decades have deepened our understanding of the role of the affective dimension (feelings) in learning. We now know, for example, that simply being in the same place that one previously experienced stress can induce new stress at levels sufficient to measure with an MRI (Cozolino, 2002). While Vygotsky (1978) called for a measure of dissonance to induce learning, we need to remember as well that what he labeled the zone of proximal development has both a lower limit or threshold and an upper limit or ceiling. Good teachers seek to push students across the threshold but they also honor the upper limit so as not to threaten students' sense of classroom safety. At its simplest, we are saying that if a catalyst metaphor leads teachers to ignore the ceiling of students' capacity for dissonance (the upper limit of Vgyotsky's zone) then those teachers need either a different metaphor or some improvement in their skills in recognizing age- and cognitive-level appropriate teaching. In fact, research into library anxiety suggests that stress beyond the upper limit of Vygotsky's zone actually causes learners to focus on their stress itself rather than on the task in front of them (Mellon, 1986). If we take seriously both recent brain research and the substantial body of research on anxiety, we will recognize the serious constraint placed on educators wishing to work with catalyst metaphors.

We have raised several cautions about catalyst metaphors. Nevertheless, just as oysters produce physical pearls after the insertion of an irritant, students often produce educational pearls after someone irritates them. Used in appropriate ways and in an appropriate mix with other approaches to teaching, catalyst teaching and learning can be a means of much learning. In our view, highly effective catalyst teachers can produce thought-provoking questions—brain freezing questions—related to all manner of subject matter, not only to the controversial and insoluble social questions raised on any given day in the news.

Conclusion

We began this chapter with a survey of some of the metaphors for teaching and learning. Then we focused on three of the main clusters of metaphors: transmission metaphors, metaphors related to guidance, coaching and facilitation, and catalyst metaphors. Our purpose has been to show how powerfully these metaphors shape our thinking about what transpires in classrooms. We hoped to show that when teachers work within any given metaphor certain ways of teaching and learning will end up in the foreground. Missing from our chapter are detailed examinations of factory and agricultural metaphors. While we did briefly note their importance, we believe that opening up just the three clusters of metaphors as we did still provides powerful insights into the power of our teaching/learning metaphors and therefore the importance of thinking carefully about them. We believe that our treatment of the three clusters we chose illustrates how important it is that educators be able to work with more than one metaphor. Bluntly, teachers know things that learners need to know; we should not apologize for viewing schools as venues to transmit a culture's heritage. Just as bluntly, as they mature, students need to take an increasing degree of responsibility for their learning, giving us a warrant for facilitation, guidance, and coaching metaphors. Teachers have a corollary responsibility in those metaphors: to plan instruction that allows students to grow into their responsibility. Such instruction implies less teacher-directed grow into this responsibility. Such instruction implies less teacher-directed transmission and more student activity and discovery. Finally, teachers must always find good ways to engage students' interest in their learning tasks. Catalyst metaphors offer a way to frame instruction that, at its best, addresses this need.

The Bible, significantly, uses all three clusters of metaphors. The first five books of the Bible, often referred to as the Torah, transmit the truth with authority and certainty. The books of wisdom such as the Proverbs are much more facilitative, presenting generalizations that call for personal thought and response for one's life, with some generalizations even being at odds with each other (e.g., Prov 26: 4–5). And in the Gospels Jesus often was a catalyst: asking questions and telling obscure stories which created dissonance in his listeners in order to elicit response. The teaching/learning relationships relationship requires more than the explicit or implicit uses of such metaphors, of course. But they do function in important ways for all teachers. As Wineberg notes in his chapter in this volume, we need a multiplicity of images to work effectively as educators. So we end with this question: What cluster of metaphors anchors the teaching/learning relationships in your classroom?

References

Anderson, D. W. (2011). Hospitable classrooms: biblical hospitality and inclusive education. *Journal of Education & Christian Belief, 15*(1), 13–27.

Austin, K. P. (2000). *Coaching as a metaphor for teaching in a community of practice.* Unpublished doctoral dissertation, Stanford University, Palo Alto, CA.

Bennett, J. (2003). *Academic life: Hospitality, ethics and spirituality.* Eugene, OR: Wipf and Stock.

Cozolino, L. J. (2002). *The neuroscience of psychotherapy: Building and rebuilding the human brain.* New York: Norton.

Efron, S., & Joseph, P. B. (2001). Reflections in a mirror: Metaphors of teachers and teaching. In P. B. Joseph & G. E. Burnaford (Eds.), *Images of schoolteachers in America* (pp. 75–91). Mahwah, NJ: Lawrence Erlbaum.

Fenwick, T. (1996). *Firestarters and outfitters: Metaphors of adult education.* Paper presented at the Canadian Society for the Study of Education, St. Catherine's ON. ERIC: ED400463.

Fischer, J., & Kiefer, A. (2001). Constructing and discovering images of your teaching. In P. B. Joseph & G. E. Burnaford (Eds.), *Images of schoolteachers in America* (pp. 93–114). Mahwah, NJ: Lawrence Erlbaum.

Graves, S. M. (2006). Dr. Coach: A metaphor to teach by. Retrieved from *Exchanges: The Online Journal of Teaching and Learning in the CSU* at http://www.calstate.edu/ITL/exchanges/index.html

Illich, I. (1970). *Deschooling society.* New York: Harper and Row.

Illich, I. (1977). Disabling professions. In I. Illich, I. K. Zola, J. McKnight, J. Caplan & H. Syhaiken (Eds.), *Disabling professions* (pp. 11–39). London: Marion Boyars.

Kuhn, T. (1970). *The structure of scientific revolutions*. Chicago, IL: University of Chicago Press.

Lakoff, G., & Johnson, M. (1980). *Metaphors we live by*. Chicago, Illinois: University of Chicago Press.

McAvoy, J. (1998). Hospitality: A feminist theology of education. *Teaching Theology and Religion, 1*(1), 20–26.

McKenzie, J. (1998). The wired classroom (continued). Retrieved from *From Now On: The Educational Technology Journal*, 7(6) at http://fno.org/mar98/flotilla2.html

Mellon, C. A. (1986). Library anxiety: A grounded theory and its development. *College & Research Libraries, 47*(2), 160–165.

Palmer, P. (1998). *The courage to teach*. San Francisco: Jossey-Bass.

Rechtschaffen, D. (2011, February). Mindful kids: Inner awareness brings calm and well-being. *Natural Awakenings, Portland Metro Edition*, 18–19.

Reinsmith, W. A. (1992). *Archetypal forms in teaching*. Westport, CT: Greenwood Press.

Rogers, C. R. (1969). *Freedom to learn*. Columbus, OH: Merrill.

Santoro Gomez, D. A. (2005). *The space for good teaching*. Unpublished doctoral dissertation, Columbia University, New York.

Santoro Gomez, D. A. (2006). The need to develop independent intelligence: The roles and responsibilities of teacher educators. *Teacher Education and Practice 19*(4), 483–501.

Scheffler, I. (1964). *The language of education*. Springfield, Il: Thomas.

Vygotsky, L. S. (1978). Interaction between learning and development (M. Cole, Trans.). In M. Cole, V. John-Steiner, S. Scribner & E. Souberman (Eds.), *Mind and society: The development of higher psychological processes* (pp. 79–91). Cambridge, MA: Harvard University Press.

Zachariah, M. (1985). Lumps of clay and growing plants: Dominant metaphors of the role of education in the Third World, 1950–1980. *Comparative Education Review, 29*(1), 1–21.

five

Curriculum as a Journey Toward Wisdom

Elaine Brouwer

THE NUMBER OF FREQUENTLY occurring curriculum metaphors reveals the variety and complexity of the curriculum field. No two people seem to want the same thing (Connelly & Clandinin, 1988, p. 73). Some curriculum metaphors are mechanistic: curriculum as a catalogue, either of topics, discrete tasks, or concepts. Others are dynamic and organic: curriculum as garden. Some are relational: curriculum as student-teacher interactions and relationship. Others imply that curriculum is a one way street or a race course, something to be received by the learner: curriculum as a course of study to be completed. Some portray curriculum as an objective thing, fixed and definable: curriculum as a well-defined, detailed core for learning. Yet others see it as a much more profound idea: curriculum as theological text.

Curriculum metaphors function in a variety of ways. They reveal our view of knowledge, our goals of teaching and learning, and the role of curriculum in realizing such goals. They also communicate the expectations we have of various players in the educational process (Smith & Shortt, 2002, p. 120). Curriculum metaphors suggest criteria for selecting and organizing content as well as the process of implementation. They influence how teachers and students interact with content and with each other. They point to preferred assessment and evaluation practices. They lean toward particular classroom arrangements and attitudes toward use of time. Metaphors for curriculum can bring into focus features that may otherwise go unnoticed (Smith & Carvill, 2000, p. 83). Metaphors are generative and dialogue-engendering. They help us "see what we don't see" (Doll, 1993, p. 169). No one metaphor is sufficient to provide a coherent and comprehensive understanding of reality, but a set of metaphors can paint a fuller picture of how we view life in the classroom (Lakoff & Johnson, 1980, p. 89).

We can also use metaphors to intentionally introduce "turbulence" into otherwise taken-for-granted ways of thinking and acting (Blomberg, 2007, p. 144). Metaphors used in that manner include curriculum as assembly line (Smith & Shortt, 2002, p. 78), as cultural bomb (Slattery, 2006, p. 73), as mailbox pigeon holes (Orr, 1994, p. 94), as a script to be executed (Wiggins & McTighe, 2007, p. 55), as a clockwork (Doll & Gough, 2002, p. 5), as haunted by the ghost of control (Doll & Gough, 2002, p. 34), as "bewitching" language of psychological and behavioral sciences (Huebner, 1999, p. 404).

Five Clusters of Curriculum Metaphors

In this section I discuss five clusters of curriculum metaphors. The clusters are not definitive categories, but represent various orientations to curriculum. There are points of overlap and agreement among them. There are also sometimes sharp differences, even within the clusters. It is important to remember that metaphors suggest. They do not prescribe.

The first cluster of metaphors organizes around the idea of producing literate citizens who can contribute to an "ecumenical national culture" (Hirsch, 1996, p. 238) of students prepared to enter into the ongoing conversation of great minds down through the ages (Bauer, 2009; Wilson, 1991), and the systematic training of the minds of children so they can become mature, rational, informed adults who can make their own judgments (VanDamme, 2006). There is also a 'container' metaphor at work in each of these approaches. Hirsch draws from a fund of common or core knowledge. Teachers in Core Knowledge schools have access to a daily planner which provides them with a comprehensive and explicit guide to implementing the Core Knowledge Sequence in their classrooms. Classical education selects its content and processes from the classics. And the container for VanDamme (2006) is her hierarchy of knowledge. Generally, this cluster of metaphors uses the technical language of goals, objectives, content, methods, and summative assessment. The intended curriculum takes precedence over the enacted or the experienced curriculum.

The second cluster of metaphors considers curriculum as a "course for getting there," in line with the original meaning of curriculum as a running or race course, with built in "speed bumps" to check for course correction (Wiggins & McTighe, 2007). Another suggested by Wiggins and McTighe is an engaging and effective itinerary derived from a prior decision about destination. A similar image is a dynamic series of planned learning experiences, or a path that sets out toward a common vision of life (Van Brummelen, 2002). This is a path that teachers and students modify as they go. A plan teachers make for the conduct of the teacher-student relationship is an image of a systematic approach to selecting and delivering learning experiences using criteria for the kind of knowledge that the school seeks to promote. In this image, curriculum is religious vision because the direction of the teacher-student relationship is set by the school's vision and objectives (Stronks & Blomberg, 1993). In these metaphors, the enacted curriculum tends to take precedence over the intended curriculum.

Curriculum as storytelling is the third cluster. Kieran Egan (1986) says that curriculum should be viewed as a story told by teachers. His emphasis is not on fictional stories but on employing the story form to teach any content more meaningfully and engagingly. The story form is powerful because it draws on "children's imaginations . . . the most powerful and energetic learning tools" (p. 2). A story-like rhythm requires a beginning that employs conflict or a dramatic tension that sets up an expectation and a conclusion that satisfies that expectation. Curriculum as story telling unites cognitive and affective meaning. Smith and Shortt's primary concern is for the big stories (meta-narratives) that the curriculum tells, implicitly or explicitly (Smith & Shortt, 2002). Depending on the organization and presentation of curricular materials, students could be hearing such big stories as the glories of technological progress, the joy of consumption, the overriding importance of economic utility, or the dangers of environmental degradation. Two stories may contain the same ingredients, but patterned differently tell divergent stories: "Change the shape of the story and the underlying message shifts" (Smith and Shortt, 2002, p. 86).

The fourth cluster includes metaphors of liberation and emancipation. Curriculum can liberate students from docility, receptivity, and obedience to past authority (Henderson & Hawthorne, 2000), and can emancipate students from domination and oppression (McLaren, 1994).

According to such thinkers, curriculum is a moral commitment and a political activity. It can transform students into "people who can think for themselves, who can engage life imaginatively and fully as life-long learners, and who can embrace democracy as a vibrant way of living" (Henderson & Hawthorne, 2000, p. 5). Curriculum is an introduction to a particular form of life. It serves to prepare students for a dominant or subservient position in existing society by favoring certain forms of knowledge over others. It affirms the dreams, aspirations, and values of some groups of students while marginalizing forms of knowledge favored by others of differing genders, classes, or races (McLaren, 1994). An emancipatory curriculum thus creates the conditions for students' self-empowerment as active political and moral subjects.

In the fifth cluster, metaphors of courtship, conversation, dance, encounter, spiritual journey, and co-journeyers can be both explicit and implicit. This group of metaphors is the furthest removed from the taken-for-granted notion of curriculum as subject matter. For instance, David Orr says that if we organized education and curriculum to correspond to the way we actually sense the world, we might have departments of sky, landscape, water, wind, sounds, time, seashores, swamps, rivers, dirt, trees, animals and "perhaps one of Ecstacy" (1994, p. 94). Students should enter into a courtship with the natural world. They should explore the mysterious and unknowable before they are introduced to the disciplines (mailbox pigeon holes) that are "abstractions organized for intellectual convenience" (Orr, p. 96).

Reality is essentially communal, says Parker Palmer. It is a "great web of being," a "dance of communal collaboration" (Palmer, 1998, p. 96). We know reality only by being in community with it ourselves, by conversing with it. The conversation begins when we put the great things (not texts, or theories, or disciplines, but the things themselves) at the center of our attention and give them the respect and authority that we normally give to human beings. The conversation deepens when we open ourselves to an "eternal dance of intimacy and distance, of speaking and listening, of knowing and not knowing" (p. 106). The subjects, the things themselves, continually call us deeper into their secrets, refusing to be reduced to our conclusions about them.

Dwayne Huebner, in "Education and Spirituality," says that we live in a universe that is fuller, deeper, stranger, more mysterious and complex than we can ever hope to know (Huebner, 1999). There is a "moreness" to every human being and to that which we experience in the world (p. 403). Using the language of goals and objectives to depict a process by which an individual moves from one state of being to another with new competencies or capacities (learning) hides the fact that our possibilities are ever before us because the transcendent, the Spirit, dwells within us. Life is movement, change, or journey. Learning too quickly explains and simplifies that journey. Education, and specifically curriculum, is a spiritual journey.

William E. Doll Jr. calls for a rethinking of the very nature of curriculum because our understanding of the world is changing. We are developing a cosmic and interrelational consciousness due to findings in quantum physics, microbiology, organic chemistry, and astrophysics (Doll, 1993a; Doll & Gough, 2002). In the field of education this new understanding points toward curriculum as a verb, not as noun: it is a process. In curriculum as process, teachers and students explore what is unknown and through that exploration "clear the land" together resulting in the transformation of the land and themselves. Learning and understanding come through dialogue and reflection, not transmission. Central to curriculum as process is the principle of self-organization versus change through external force.

Karen Baptist (2002) explores the notion of garden as a metaphor for curriculum. Both garden and curriculum are social constructs that reflect the intents of the maker and prevailing cultural ideologies. Experience in both is a synthesis of orchestrated and life-world experiences. Both honor the senses and engage the body. The garden and curriculum as garden connect us to ourselves, our communities, and to the earth. Curriculum as garden is a dance of control and release with shifting interactions between teacher, learner, and text that opens up possibilities. It is a garden that encourages and celebrates multiple ways of knowing and that educates students to live well where they are.

Patrick Slattery (2006) believes that education should be committed to advancing a just, compassionate, and ecologically sustainable global community. It should be a "prophetic enterprise that seeks justice" (p. xvi). Curriculum, then, should be a public discourse that seeks transformation. Recognizing that religion and spirituality are powerful forces in the lives of individuals, capable of inspiring moves toward justice or injustice, Slattery proposes that the study of religion and spirituality should have a prominent place in curriculum discourse. He calls this exploration of religion, spirituality, and culture in their complex manifestations "theology"—not to be confused with sectarian religious debates or denominational sectarianism (Blomberg, 2007, p. 105). The goal of curriculum as theological text is the getting of wisdom, not information transmission. Curriculum should be a "healing curriculum dance" (p. 2) that is not restricted to the modern program of studies codified in textbooks, curriculum guides, scope and sequences, and behavioral lesson plans. Instead, the mystical, multicultural, interdisciplinary, social, ecological, and holistic all become part of the curriculum.

Slattery uses "curriculum," "theological," and "text" in their verb forms. Curriculum is running the race, *currere*, a process. Theology is seeking, an "autobiographical process, a cosmological dialogue, and a search for personal and universal harmony." Practiced as process, theology situates the individual between the "already" and the "not yet" in an unfolding history with God "ahead" rather than "above" (p. 93). The encounter between "text" and reader closely resembles the Latin *ruminare*, to ruminate or think things over (p. 93-94). Meaning is something readers make out of what they find in the text. "Curriculum," "theology," and "text" are primarily verbs that imply running, seeking, and ruminating.

Curriculum, says Doug Blomberg (2007), is a processing by students and teacher. It is a tool in the hands for the getting of wisdom. Experiences are selected and organized according to what is of most value, the kinds of learnings that lead to a flourishing human life. This is a wisdom curriculum best understood in active and relational terms—as verb, preposition, and adjective rather than noun. Curriculum in its verb form is what teachers and students do together. Curriculum as a preposition (from Latin—"place before") suggests that the enacted curriculum is a relationship in time between teacher, student, and pedagogical intent. Curriculum as adjective is a "painting of the world in miniature" (p. 125). It is a conscious reordering of the world for the purposes of teaching and learning, shaped by the ends toward which teaching and learning are directed.

Each of the five clusters discussed above rests on an understanding of the nature of reality which influences the choice and organization of content, the *what* of curriculum. Each also answers the *why* question of teaching and learning, shaped by the ends toward which teaching and learning are directed. The *how* of curriculum implementation varies from metaphor to metaphor due to the user's understanding of the nature of human beings and their relationship to the world. Issues of the what, why, and how of curriculum rest on personal, deeply held, sometimes only partially understood convictions. Because we teach who we are (Palmer, 1998), the task for each of us is to choose the metaphor(s) that leans into and embodies our worldview. The metaphors that speak most poignantly to me are those that see creation as a marvelous, mysterious, continuous outpouring of God's love (made sick by human rebellion). Metaphors that point to the call to live as fully human beings who are to carry forth the redemptive work of Jesus resonate with me. And I am inspired by metaphors that open up thoughts of a universe-wide, dynamic harmony described by biblical writers as *shalom*.

In the next section, I will look more closely at the metaphors of curriculum as plan or path, curriculum as process, curriculum as garden, and curriculum as a tool for the getting of wisdom. As you read, consider what each metaphor helps you see that you might not otherwise have seen or considered. Dialogue with the text to sharpen your own metaphor or set of metaphors. Then consider the fit of your chosen metaphor(s) with your personal worldview.

Curriculum as Plan or Path

The metaphors of a "course for getting there" (Wiggins & McTighe, 2007), a dynamic series (path) of planned learning experiences (Van Brummelen, 2002), and a plan that teachers make for the conduct of the teacher-student relationship (Stronks & Blomberg, 1993) suggest similar curricular practices.

Curriculum as plan or path implies a prior decision about destination. On the school-level, decisions about destination derive from long-term purposes of schooling related to mission or a common vision of life. Learning content is not the destination. Content and pedagogy are means to ends derived from a vantage point outside of content (Wiggins & McTighe, 2007). School mission statements, properly formulated, describe the macro-level destination of learning. Consider the following examples:

> Salem High School is a student-focused community challenged by a rigorous curriculum that fosters both critical and creative thinking. Provided with a personalized, safe learning environment, students will demonstrate higher-order reasoning skills, service to the school and community, and tolerance toward all individuals.

Each student will leave Salem High School with the tools necessary for a life-long commitment to citizenship, service, and learning. (Wiggins & McTighe, 2007, p. 16-17)

Central Station Christian Middle School, a denominationally and culturally diverse educational community, seeks to provide a secure learning environment in which students and teachers can explore and evaluate all of life under God. Recognizing a variety of student abilities, it aims to uncover and develop the unique giftedness of each student so that he or she may become a follower of Jesus Christ who is a faithful and creative servant of God and neighbor and steward of His world. (Stronks & Blomberg, 1993, p. 72)

On the unit-level, decisions about destination rest on a careful selection of what is enduring or essential in a unit of study and on worthy, authentic student performances that would demonstrate understanding of the essentials. Consider this abridged example from a grade 5-8 science unit (Wiggins and McTighe, 2004, p. 32):

Enduring understandings:

- A balance must exist in the environment that should allow for clean air, fresh water, and soil capable of producing food.
- All people are responsible for maintaining the balance.
- Wetlands must be protected to maintain clean water.
- Each citizen can take action to maintain a clean water supply.

Performance task:

- As a member of a research team, gather environmental evidence about your site and develop a case study for the Nature Conservancy which has received a grant to present both economic and environmental issues to the general population.

Arrival at destination will not happen if the students don't travel the path or work the plan. Students must actively participate if they are to demonstrate understanding. Therefore, students need to be invited to join the teacher on the path, to work with the teacher to accomplish the plan. In the backward design process of Wiggins and McTighe's *Understanding by Design*, the invitation is extended by posing intriguing essential questions, questions that by their nature invite immediate engagement.

Van Brummelen advocates a four-phase model of learning to engage students. The four phases—setting the stage, disclosure, reformulation, and transcendence—provide for a variety of learning styles and profiles. He cites an example from an introduction to a unit on the Renaissance. The teacher set the stage by beginning with an intriguing puzzle: What do these paintings (a Renaissance and a post-Renaissance painting) portray? Setting the stage is followed by more formal disclosure as students read, research, and discuss. To show their growing understanding, students reformulate their ideas in writing using related vocabulary. Then, finally, the students personalize their learning by drawing a picture (Van Brummelen, 2002).

If the guide provides only a list of places to visit, arrival at a destination may not happen. Arrival is more likely if those involved have an engaging and effective itinerary. Teachers need to provide a blueprint that communicates to everyone concerned, including the student, a picture of the end in mind. From these blueprints, curriculum practitioners develop coherent, logical work plans in support of a common long term goal. Architects, moviemakers, chefs, lawyers, and doctors who are focused on achieving very specific effects adjust plans to ensure the results sought. Teachers must do the same. Similarly, the teacher must plan teaching and learning activities that will help students come to understanding and successfully complete a performance task.

A dynamic plan implies that the plan or path may need to change. To assess for the need for adjustment, the teacher deliberately plans for speed bumps or checkpoints that slow down the process, allowing for checks for understanding and course correction. The speed bumps or checkpoints take the form of assessment for learning, feedback for teacher and students on how things are going. A path is not traveled relentlessly. Breaks for rest and refreshment allow the traveler to maintain the stamina needed to reach the destination. Complex plans require that the workers step back to renew their vision of the whole. Speed bumps or check points provide opportunities for reflection and renewal. Journals or learning logs, guided conversations, think-pair-share, and exit cards are examples of productive check points.

Curriculum as Process

We need to play with the idea of curriculum to understand curriculum as process. It is a very different concept than the notion of curriculum as an almost universal, linear course to be run with a definite beginning, middle, and end, a conception firmly embodied in traditional school structures and procedures. Instead, curriculum as process is a "complex web of interactions evolving naturally into more varied interconnected forms" (Doll & Gough, 2002, p. 46). It acknowledges the complexity and relatedness of all commonplaces of education, self included.

Curriculum as process is more kaleidoscopic than telescopic or microscopic (Slattery, 2006). Complex phenomena such as weather or a tree, for instance, cannot be properly studied under a microscope. Microscopes and telescopes fragment and isolate. They cannot see the whole: "An individual tree is the result of a vast, shifting set of unique circumstances, a kaleidoscope of influences such as gravity, magnetic fields, soil composition, wind, sun angles, insect hordes, human harvesting, other trees, [and] continuously active forces, facts too numerous to determine in detail" (Briggs as cited in Slattery, 2006, p. 283). To experience the kaleidoscopic complexity, students need to be immersed in fruitful experience long before they are exposed to someone else's conclusions. They need space and time to become attentive and alert, to discover and make meaning. They require greater use of theme and issue-based interdisciplinary studies to counter the fragmentation and abstraction of disciplines and departments.

According to Doll and Gough (2002), curriculum as *currere* should be filled with enough ambiguity, challenge, and unstated assumptions to invite the student into multilayers of interpretation and meaning. Students should strive towards a sense of coherence and integration that was not there when the struggle began. An example of curriculum that honors the complexity of reality and asks students to dialogue with and ruminate over that complexity is a high school oral history project described by Slattery (2006). The goal of the project was to allow students to construct an oral history in the community that could be used in the local antebellum plantation museum. Of particular concern to the project organizers was that the names of plantation owners were visible in the museum, but the enslaved were only mentioned on one plaque as having lived in the slave quarters. The names of the enslaved were known in the community, however. It was the students' task to reconstruct and reinterpret the history of the plantation through interviews and artifacts. Such a project provides an opportunity to explore a historical event from multiple perspectives such as the historical, racial, autobiographical, and philosophical. This project highlights another important feature of curriculum as process. It begins with the local and contextual before it broadens out to the larger picture. It also asks the student to reconsider the past, which then affects the present, and creates possibilities for the future.

Curriculum as process is a conversation that calls teachers and students to respect, honor, and understand their own humanness and the "otherness" of each other as well as the texts studied. Students are encouraged to enter into "actual lived situations" (Doll & Gough, 2002, p. 48). They are invited to converse with what they encounter and to be alert to the "moreness" in ourselves, others, and the world (Huebner, 1999, p. 403). Being alert to this "moreness" is akin to being hospitable to the stranger (Smith & Carvill, 2000). Hospitality to the stranger, the other—be that person or nonperson—requires a loving, welcoming, humble disposition. Teachers aiming to cultivate such a disposition might use simulations or activities in which teachers ask students to step into the shoes of another person or thing and then ask them to explain what they as that character thought and felt.

In curriculum as process the teacher's role is very important, not as external control or enforcer, but as facilitator and guide. The teacher leads from within, not as a dictator from without. Questions of procedures, methodologies, and values are always local decisions involving students, teachers, and local mores and traditions. The teacher is "first among equals" (Doll, 1993, p. 166). Community is the "organizational glue" that holds this approach to curriculum together. Experiences that transform are not private affairs. The human community, nested within the cultural which in turn is nested within the ecological and cosmological and rooted in care and critique, is the vehicle by which we transcend and transform ourselves (Doll & Gough, 2002).

Classrooms using a process approach to curriculum are less likely to have an obvious front. Desks or tables are more likely to be arranged in a seminar circle (Doll, 1993, p. 166) or some other arrangement that allows for students to see each other and the teacher. Teachers would choose technologies that allow for creative and critical interaction among students as well as between students and teacher. The classroom environment would be safe and unhurried (Doll, 1993, p. 166).

Curriculum as process is always most concerned with the kind of persons teacher and students become. The transformation of self, others, and the world and journeying toward wisdom and justice are more important than the knowledge acquired. The journey of transformation is a life-long process, "an eternal conversation" (Palmer, 1998, p. 104). The destination always lies ahead.

Curriculum as Garden

Karen Baptist helps us to rethink curriculum by spinning a web of meaning between garden and curriculum (Baptist, 2002). Curriculum as garden reminds us that outside elements such as sun and rain cannot be shut out of the system. Similarly there are outside elements that cannot be kept out of the learning space. Each student and teacher brings with them the varied elements of their life-worlds. These life-worlds include home experiences, effects of previous schooling, social and cultural factors, race and ethnicity. In curriculum as garden these factors are not treated as hurdles to overcome. They are regarded as essential for a rich curriculum experience. In the garden each season brings different conditions, providing opportunities to imagine possibilities, to experiment, and to try new varieties of seed. If the gardener tries to completely control the "event" of the garden, possibilities may never emerge. Similarly, in curriculum as garden, if the teacher tries to control the interaction among the life-worlds of the participants and their encounter with educational events, possibilities for growth and transformation may be lost.

Both garden and curriculum are based on nature and natural forms of knowing. At its best, curriculum mimics natural forms of learning through experiential learning modes. The fluidity of curriculum as garden allows for the flourishing of spontaneous growth. The gardener can arrest the natural processes in the garden by imposing a monoculture order, weeding out all diverse forms. Similarly, curriculum based on the imposition of power, dominance, rules, and order distorts natural ways of knowing. To avoid such practices, the teacher needs to seek a balance between controlled cultivation and unfettered growth. Curriculum can encourage "natural" life-enhancing learning by "nurturing an 'ecology of meaning' where connectivity, experience, imagination and growth dominate" (Baptist, 2002, p. 21).

Like gardens, curriculum can rekindle the spiritual nature of humankind. Attentiveness, imagination, and contemplation cultivate a spiritual consciousness of deep sensitivity and empowered action. A garden is a construction of vision and intent. So too curriculum as garden needs to be a construction of a vision of empowerment. Invasive ideologies of oppressive power and control must be weeded out.

Order provides structure to garden and to curriculum. The order that emerges is based on the sometimes unstated purpose and philosophy of the gardener. In curriculum the learner's view of the world will be shaped by how ideological patterns are put into action. Therefore, teachers must constantly seek to understand the structures and beliefs that underlie their ordering of curriculum. In curriculum as garden the order of curriculum is seen, not as documents, but as events and happenings that create realms of possibility.

Just as biodiversity is being threatened, so too is cultural diversity. Globalization and the spread of technology threaten to create a global monoculture. Curriculum as garden aims to maintain and celebrate cultural diversity through curricular forms that encourage and celebrate multiple ways of knowing. Local place is important in curriculum as garden. Learners are encouraged to begin to look for understanding within their own schools, institutions, and neighborhoods. Baptist highlights a program called "Landscapes for Learning" in which schoolyards are turned into ecological learning labs. Quoting Stine (1997), "To learn about, to value, and to ultimately protect their world, children need to experience it fully in both its natural and built forms, where process is interwoven with product" (Baptist, 2002, p. 28). Teachers encourage students to re-describe the world by highlighting that which lies beneath their feet. Students are encouraged to explore personally relevant questions. Curriculum is not viewed as the getting of knowledge but as an evolving process of self-knowledge. This allows the learner to interpret the world and be interpreted by the world through progressions of self-understanding and meaningful action.

Gardens and gardening can be healing experiences. They engage the whole person into the experience, uniting minds, bodies, and spirit. Curriculum has been too often fractured, engaging minds, but ignoring bodies and spirit in the learning experience. Whole person experiences shape us more powerfully than information. Perhaps educational encounters which seek to honor all aspects of human knowing, including the knowledge of the body can reintroduce forms of knowledge not limited to the logical-rational.

The metaphor of curriculum as garden is shaped by the interplay of the user's image of and experience with gardens and their worldview. Consequently the metaphor can lead to very different visions of education. Consider the garden images of John Amos Comenius and Jean-Jacques Rousseau.

The garden images of John Amos Comenius, a seventeenth century Moravian educator, were shaped by his experience of carefully crafted Medieval gardens and his reading of Scripture (Smith and Shortt, 2002). "Hovering behind Comenius' garden imagery is the garden of Eden as described in Genesis chapters 1-3, and in its train the whole subsequent network of garden and vineyard imagery in the Bible" (p.110–11). Comenius believed that each person was placed in a "garden of delight" to become "a garden of delight for his God" (p. 102). Indeed, the whole world is to be a garden of delight for God. Comenius' garden metaphor consists of a "network of imagery which included learners as plants, teaching as watering, learning as fruit-bearing, books as flower beds . . ." (p. 121).

For Comenius, nature is not the wilderness that our world has become, but its original condition recoverable through the process of redemption. Likewise human nature is not our sinful human condition but our original calling from which we have strayed and which must be progressively recovered and realized. Just as the gardener brings nature under discipline so it can bear greater fruit, the teacher is to plant, water and prune so the child is shaped in God-pleasing ways. Our original condition is a starting point for development that requires a teacher's formative intervention in order for the child to become a "rational, wise, virtuous, and pious creature" (p. 109). Comenius believed that careful education through the work of the Spirit could play a significant role in the process of redemption. This careful education should be both ordered and enjoyable, consisting of both discipline (cultivation) and playfulness (delight).

Jean-Jacques Rousseau's garden image points to a very different conception of curriculum and education. Rousseau preferred idyllic gardens in which natural elements were set free, perfect gardens in which humans could be their true natural selves. In *Émile*, 1762, he wrote that

"Everything is good as it leaves the hands of the author" and "Everything degenerates in the hands of man." Correspondingly, he believed that the learner was innately good and that the civilizing intervention of a teacher was a potentially damaging intrusion (p. 106). He wanted Émile to be educated with the least possible restraint. The job of his teachers was to preserve his innate goodness and to be alert to where his interests might lead so they could be prepared to guide him in a healthy direction. Émile should not be pressured into early book learning because senses and feeling were primary. His education would take place best in a rural setting rather than an urban one so the corruption of other people could be minimized (Noddings, 1998).

Curriculum as Journey Toward Wisdom

Metaphors of process, garden and theological text resonate with me. Aspects of each of these metaphors fit my understanding of the world and our place in it. The emphasis on lived experience in its wholeness and integrity as a focal point of curriculum honors our daily experience of creation, both natural and built. The active involvement of the learner as whole person—mind, body, and spirit—is consistent with my understanding of the nature of human beings and of how we learn. I am also drawn to the stress on transformation, justice, and peace because these concerns lie at the heart of God's intention for the world. Nonetheless, these metaphors are a bit illusive, perhaps necessarily so. They don't prescribe because they cannot. Working out the implications of these metaphors requires judgment and discernment, an alertness and sensitivity to context, and an imaginative and creative response.

Having acknowledged the necessity of a degree of ambiguity, I do believe that we can bring insights from these metaphors into sharper focus by couching them within the metaphor of curriculum as journey toward wisdom with *journey* and *wisdom* being the key concepts.

For a description of what constitutes wisdom I turn to several themes that emerge in an exploration of the Hebrew wisdom teachings (e.g., Brueggemann, 1982; Blomberg, 2007; and Birch, Brueggemann, Fretheim, & Peterson, 1999). Brueggemann asserts that the substance of wisdom teaching is that the human task is the formation and nurture of human community and what needs to be known for this task can be found out. Ultimately this knowing is not to discover techniques for management, but "it is finally doxology which is based on wonder, awe, and amazement" (Brueggemann, 1982, p. 84). He submits "that it is the discovery, premise, assumption, and conviction of the interconnectedness of life that is the central substance of the wisdom teachers" (p. 84). Wisdom in Israel, he says, "needs to be understood as a serious way in which responsible, reasonable knowledge of the world and passionate trust in God are held together" (p. 68). How is this wisdom learned? What are the implications of journey toward wisdom for curriculum?

First, curriculum as journey toward wisdom acknowledges that wisdom is found in the experience of the world. "The object which contains wisdom is the world, the created order" (p. 72). Wisdom is not something that can be learned in the abstract. It is not a set of universal principles that can be applied to any situation. Wisdom is situation specific. It is discipleship in the real world, in culturally situated, historically defined contexts. It is in the knowledge of the individual and particular that decisions are made and actions taken. Curriculum as journey toward wisdom does not reduce the world to manageable, disconnected bits predigested for the learner. Rather, students encounter whole things in their many-sidedness—things, plants, persons, institutions, acts, events—rather than just conclusions or abstractions about those things. A study of agriculture, for instance, should begin with an extended encounter with a local farm so that students could experience first-hand the many aspects of a farm. As students and teacher engage in a cycle of question/answer/counterquestion around the perspectives of farmers, corporations, consumers, and environmentalists, students would likely identify areas that they want to explore. The study of a local farm, then, becomes a tool in the hand to learn how to respond with wisdom to issues surrounding agriculture (Blomberg, 2007).

Second, curriculum as journey toward wisdom confesses that daily life has a shape that must be respected, discerned, and responded to (Brueggemann, 1982). "Wise living consists in respecting the 'givens' of daily life in making responsible choices about daily existence and in anticipating the consequences of those choices" (Birch et al.,1999, p. 374). God created his world so that all parts are delicately related to one another, and "therefore every decision, every act matters to the shape and well-being of the whole" (p. 376). Curriculum as a journey toward wisdom is grounded in the conviction that all of life is interconnected even when the linages are not immediately evident. It is the task of curriculum as journey toward wisdom to help students "see in the midst of seeming disorder a coherence that can be relied on" (Brueggemann, 1982, p. 81). Curriculum as journey toward wisdom invites students to explore the kaleidoscopic complexity of the world and seek to understand always more fully how the mysterious interdependence is shaped. Recognizing interdependence enables students to consider how they might live in right relationship with each other and the world. Curriculum as journey toward wisdom would be, largely, an integral curriculum. Connections are more evident in an integral curriculum than in a discipline-based approach.

Third, while some wisdom teachings can be delivered directly, the principal mode of knowing is engagement with the world which requires "fascination, imagination, patience, attentiveness to detail, and finally, observation of the regularities which seem to govern" (Brueggemann, 1982, p. 72). It requires a playful intensity that deals with the world in its integrity, "meeting it and treating it as it presents to us" (Blomberg, 2007, p. 88). Curriculum as journey toward wisdom creates spaces for learners to attend to the world "in all its playfulness, to know that what immediately meets the eye is not all there is" (Brueggemann, 1982, p.75). The purpose of such engagement is to "nurture people into the practice of discernment, of watching slowly, patiently, enduringly, to see what will be given us" (p. 74). Curriculum as journey toward wisdom must be evocative. It points to "a way of going, a manner of being, an established direction and pattern of living" (Blomberg, 2007, p. 54). To do so, it would employ such tools as inquiry and project-based learning and simulations so students have the opportunity to experience, contemplate, organize, imagine, choose, and act. Curriculum as journey toward wisdom would provide many opportunities for students to craft purposeful responses and to act on them.

Fourth, wisdom is experiential; it is not dogmatic. The wisdom teachers resisted certitudes: "They refused to settle, because they knew that after the lived experience of today, there would be tomorrow with its own insistent questions" (Birch et al., 1999, p. 415). Wisdom rests on faith, but not a settled faith. Rather, it is a faith that is "endlessly re-thought because lived experience is the grist of faith" (p. 413). Perhaps, then, wisdom can be described as "faith seeking understanding" (p. 414) in the midst of lived experiences. Curriculum as journey toward wisdom assumes a humble stance acknowledging that wisdom is found in God and not all of it is available to human kind. Yet, as Brueggemann (1982) put it, "some of it is. And that is enough for nurture, for faith, and for life" (p. 90). Curriculum as journey toward wisdom is oriented primarily toward cultivating character, toward formation rather than information (Blomberg, 2007). This requires a careful dance of cultivation and natural growth. It requires space for direct instruction and guidance, but also space for learners to explore their personal responses.

Finally, in curriculum as journey toward wisdom the destination always lies ahead. While both trip and journey refer to a course of travel to a particular place, usually for a specific purpose, a trip can be long or short, taken at either a rushed or leisurely pace. Journey, however, suggests that a considerable amount of time and distance will be covered. Learning wisdom is a life-long process, because "there is something slippery and unprogrammed about lived reality" (Birch et al., 1999, p. 393). Sometimes present lived experience does not conform to older taken-for-granted commitments. The wisdom teachers were "endlessly preoccupied with making ethical sense out of a lived world that is endlessly under-estimated and recalcitrant" (p. 396). Wisdom is not knowledge received once and for all, but "knowing in ongoing process." It is a continual and dynamic repositioning of oneself in relation to other things (Blomberg, 2007, p. 129). It is the task of curriculum as journey toward wisdom to equip young people to take this journey.

Various models can serve us well in putting shape to curriculum as journey toward wisdom. Two of them were mentioned earlier in this chapter—the three stage approach of *Understanding by Design* (Wiggins and McTighe, 2004) and Van Brummelen's four phases of learning (Van Brummelen, 2002). Blomberg (2007) offers yet another model that may be a "small place to begin" (p. 179) for teachers who want to craft curriculum as journey toward wisdom. Play, problem posing, and purposeful response, he says, are three moments that permeate our everyday experience. Play is an engaging, active encounter with aspects of God's creation. Reading a book just to enjoy it before engaging in critical analysis, stepping into a painting so that it becomes a world in itself, encountering mathematical questions in planning a building project are all examples of that engaging, active encounter. Problem posing suggests that "our experience of creation is deepened . . . by addressing questions to/that arise from [play]" (p.180). What does this mean? What ought I do? Why did this happen? Problems invite purposeful responses. This moment in our experiencing of the world underscores that most important in the encounter is normative action, not detached contemplation of propositional truths. Purposeful response is a move toward maturity, toward growing in wisdom. Taken together, these three moments can lead to the formation of persons who not only know the right thing to do in a situation, but who are disposed to do it. Attending to these moments opens up space for the learner to move from who they are now (which is not who they were) to who they will become. Blomberg proposes this model not as an algorithm but as an evocative way of thinking about learning as transformation or growth in wisdom. While it may be helpful to think in these terms as we plan curriculum, it is important to remember that they are moments that permeate each other, not compartments (p.181).

Crafting curriculum as journey toward wisdom is hard, weighty work. It takes wisdom and discernment to choose and organize experiences and texts that have the potential of opening up possibilities for learnings that lead to a flourishing human life. It requires alertness and flexibility to reshape the curriculum as students and teacher listen to each other and attend closely to that which they are experiencing and studying. Yes, it is hard work, but it can also be playful, delightful work if we remain alive to the mystery of growing in wisdom and maintain a stance of "imaginative 'ad hochishness'" (Brueggemann, 1982, p. 80).

Conclusion

Metaphors help us "see what we don't see" (Doll, 1993, p. 169), but no one metaphor can do justice to the complexity of the curriculum field. The metaphors of garden, process, theological text, and journey are all helpful to me in their own way in aligning my views of curriculum with my worldview. However, what makes each of them richer is the answer to the question "But where shall wisdom be found?" (Job 28:12)

It is very important to choose curriculum metaphors that align with our worldview because metaphors have "material effects" (Norman Fairclough as cited in Doll & Gough, 2002, p. 73). Our metaphors for curriculum determine the very character of the relationship of the teacher and students in the learning space (Blomberg, 2007). They privilege one view of life and the world over others. If a set of metaphors gains traction, it can lead to pervasive shifts in practice (Smith & Shortt, 2002). We are, therefore, responsible for the effects of the metaphors we privilege (Norman Fairclough as cited in Doll & Gough, 2002, p. 74).

References

Bauer, S. Wise (2009). *The well trained mind: Classical education for the next generation* (rev. ed.). Charles City, VA: Peace Hill Press.

Baptist, Karen (2002). The garden as metaphor for curriculum. *Teacher Education Quarterly 29* (4), 19–37, retrieved on 4/15/09 from http://findarticles.com/p/articles/mi_qa3960/is_200210/ai_n9121971/?tag=content;col1.

Birch, B., Brueggemann, W., Fretheim, T., & Petersen, D. (1999). *A theological introduction to the Old Testament.* Nashville, TN: Abingdon Press.

Blomberg, D. (2007). *Wisdom and curriculum: Christian schooling after postmodernity.* Sioux Center, IA: Dordt College Press.

Brueggemann, W., (1982). *The creative word: Canon as a model for biblical education.* Philadelphia, PA: Fortress Press.

Connellly, F. M. & Clandinin, J. (1988). *Teachers as curriculum planners: Narratives of experience.* New York: Teachers College Press.

Doll, W. Jr (1993). *A post-modern perspective on curriculum.* New York: Teachers College Press.

Doll, W. & Gough, N. (Eds.). (2002). *Curriculum visions.* New York: Peter Lang.

Egan, K. (1986). *Teaching as story telling.* London, ON: Althouse.

Henderson, J. & Hawthorne, R. (2000). *Transformative curriculum leadership* (2nd ed.). Upper Saddle River, NJ: Merrill.

Hirsch, E.D. Jr. (1996). *The schools we need: Why we don't have them.* New York: Doubleday.

Huebner, D. (1999). Education and spirituality. In V. Hillis (Ed.), *The lure of the transcendent: Collected essays of Dwayne Huebner.* (pp. 401–416). Mahwah, NJ: Lawrence Erlbaum.

Lakoff, G. & Johnson, M. (1980/2003). *Metaphors we live by.* Chicago, IL: University of Chicago Press.

McLaren, P. (1994). *Life in schools: An introduction to critical pedagogy in the foundations of education.* Toronto, ON: Irwin.

Noddings, N. (1998). *Philosophy of education.* Boulder, CO: Westview Press.

Orr, D. (1994). *Earth in mind: On education, environment, and the human prospect.* Washington DC: Island Press.

Palmer, P. (1998). *The courage to teach: Exploring the inner landscape of a teacher's life.* San Francisco, CA: John Wiley.

Slattery, P. (2006). *Curriculum development in the postmodern era* (2nd ed.). New York: Routledge.

Smith, D. & Carvill, B. (2000). *The gift of the stranger: Faith, hospitality, and foreign language learning.* Grand Rapids, MI: Eerdmans.

Smith, D. & Shortt, J. (2002). *The Bible and the task of teaching.* Nottingham, UK: Stapleford Center.

Stronks, G., and Blomberg, D. (Eds.). (1993). *A vision with a task: Christian schooling for responsive discipleship.* Grand Rapids, MI: Baker Books.

Van Brummelen, H. (2002). *Steppingstones to curriculum: A biblical path.* Colorado Springs, CO: Purposeful Design.

VanDamme, L. (2006). The hierarchy of knowledge: the most neglected issue in education. *The Objective Standard: A Journal of Culture and Politics 1*(1), 55-81. Retrieved at http://www.theobjectivestandard.com/back-issues.asp.

Wiggins, G. & McTighe, J. (2004). *Understanding by design: Professional development workbook.* Alexandria, VA: Association for Supervision and Curriculum Development.

Wiggins, G. & McTighe, J. (2007). *Schooling by design: Mission, action, and achievement.* Alexandria, VA: Association for Supervision and Curriculum Development.

Wilson, D. (1991). *Recovering the lost tools of learning: An approach to distinctively Christian education.* Wheaton, IL: Crossway Books.

six

Student Assessment:
Hitting the Mark or Lighting the Candle?

Harro Van Brummelen

MY CAREER AS EDUCATOR has spanned more than four decades. During this time, little has been as difficult or as painful as assessing students. On my latest (university) student course evaluations my scores for "value of feedback" and "return time of feedback on assignments" were very close to the "perfect" 4.0 mark. I gave formative feedback on several drafts that "didn't count." And students had to use my summative feedback as well as in-class peer assessment on their major projects to submit a take-home final examination question as to how they could improve their projects. The same day I discussed assignment expectations in class, I also posted the assessment rubric on my course website.

However, at the end of the course I still asked myself: Had I incorporated enough self- and peer-assessment for optimal learning? Was my extensive evening and weekend time worth the benefit for students? Was I being totally fair when I gave all students in a cluster whose total scores were between 78.9% and 80.9% a B+ even though our official cut-off is 80.0%? More importantly, how did my assessment affect how these future teachers view assessment? I want them to think of it in terms of assessment *for* and *as* learning. But they are very much aware that they need a B- average grade to be accepted into the last year of our teacher education program. So do they still see assessment mainly as a way to sort the sheep from the goats? Certainly one student thought so: she regularly came to see me when a mark was not quite what she had hoped. And I had to admit several times that my response—even when I used a detailed rubric—was defensible but nevertheless subjective. Another instructor (or myself at a different time or under different circumstances) might well have come up with a somewhat different score. Nor could I avoid that my final grade was a judgment. In essence I told students with 69% (C+) or lower that they would not make suitable teachers. Yet a grade of 70% (B-) or higher affirmed them as future teachers. I can tell my students that I'm assessing their work, and not them. But their perception often still is, "This is what you think I am worth." I am not the only one who struggles with the issues swirling around student assessment: Lorna Earl reports that during her thirty years of working with teachers, they routinely told her that "assessment is the hardest part" (2003, p. ix).

Perhaps assessment is so difficult because it can and does have negative consequences, and therefore elicits negative student response. Chris McKillop (2006) asked 86 undergraduate and postgraduate university students to represent visually how they felt about assessment, without the term being discussed with them. The common themes that emerged were frustration, being judged, feeling uncomfortable, and perplexity. They thought of assessment as a formal, summative process. Half the students drew negative emotions such as discomfort and pain. Only five of the 86 expressed any positive feelings. Metaphorical representations of assessment included students cringing in a corner with shaded figures laughing at them; being a rat in a maze; having a gun pointed at their head; climbing a steep staircase with sharp edges and clouds darkening the way; having the weight of the world on their shoulders; and hanging from gallows when taking an exam.

Such feelings are not limited to university students. I have observed primary students who were devastated by a preponderance of negative teacher comments in their journals. I also remember my own high school where immense pressure to do well on tests resulted in three of the four top students in the province coming from that (small) school in my graduation year, but where it also led to a group of students burning the principal in effigy in a tree in front of the school. Often students view assessment as one-sided judgment—as an unfair or inscrutable verdict or sentence.

Whether we admit it or not, assessment in schools drives instruction. It wags the tail of learning. It shapes students' dispositions, values, and attitudes—their view of what is important in life. It shows students what the system and society value, and what they therefore should value.

It also affects personal relationships in the classroom. If you want to change learning, then you must change assessment.

I do believe that a large proportion of teachers, particularly but not solely at the elementary school level, are trying to ensure that their assessment supports and promotes student learning. They do their best to create assessment that is affirming rather than judgmental. Many schools have developed assessment policies and strategies that emphasize helping students to improve. However, such attempts are often undermined by high-stakes testing that ranks schools, teachers, and students, or by a strong focus on summative assessment of tests and assignments. How we approach and how we implement assessment in schools is often rooted in the metaphors about teaching, learning, and assessment that teachers or that society explicitly or implicitly accept. And some of those metaphors have been at war with each other in North American education during the past two decades.

Education-Related Metaphors that Affect Assessment

Through metaphors we experience one thing in terms of another, sometimes in surprising and original ways. As such, metaphors related to assessment can enrich our understanding and have the power to shape our view of student assessment and evaluation.[1] They can open up discourse about the meaning and purpose of assessment. Metaphors lead to new perspectives. Their imagery can be a creative tool that sheds light on assessment. If we are aware of their presence and power, they lead to self-reflection about how they enrich our assessment insight and practice. At the same time, assessment metaphors can also limit us and serve as blinders that restrain us from seeing its deficiencies and incompleteness. They break down if pushed too far since no assessment metaphor equals assessment itself. Yet they often help us to transcend the functional and technical aspects of assessment that have so often dominated the literature. For all these reasons it is useful to consider how metaphors of as-

---

1. Student assessment is generally understood as the gathering of data about achievement in learning; evaluation, as the interpretation of such data with respect to the extent to which learning outcomes have been achieved, strengths and weaknesses in students' learning, etc. However, the boundary between the two terms is often unclear, and the terms, especially in the past, have been used interchangeably, as, for instance, in a book such as Fenwick and Parson's *The Art of Evaluation* (2009).

sessment as well as other educational metaphors influence how we view, develop, and implement classroom assessment.

Interestingly, the number of explicit metaphors used to describe student assessment is not all that large. What occurs more often is that educators show how metaphors for various commonplaces in education have implications for assessment. For instance, Christopher Ormell (1996) compares how some look at education as a process of chewing and digesting, while others prefer the metaphor of opening the eyes of the child as a result of reaching the top of a mountain. The implication for the chewing and digesting metaphor is that assessment must be linear and thorough. But for the mountaintop vista metaphor, assessment focuses on meaningful observation, retrospection, and synthesis that lead to deeper insight. Similarly, if we view schools as factories (or students as blank slates), student variation tends to be stamped out and "we would have well-established processes to measure and assess the quality of each product as it came off the assembly line" (Theobald, 2009, p. 2). But if schools are thought of as gardens (or students as unfolding plants), we attempt to make classrooms "places of refuge, creation, and restoration" (Theobald, 2009, p. 2), with students being assessed in terms of their personal rate of development and learning styles, and our assessment providing for and honoring their diversity. Somewhere in between are educators who look at learning as a journey or as a road trip. For them, assessment becomes formative monitoring, but where students, nevertheless, are expected to end up at the same destination (Deacon Crick, 2007; Tuttle, 2009). And at least one author claims that if schools are seen as jazz groups with purposive school leadership reflecting the improvisional style of jazz, then school leaders will be able to meet "the spiritual imperative to guiding schools beyond the high-stakes testing and minimum proficiency" so that they will be able "to create in order to reconstruct" (Dantley, 2003, p. 273 & 290).

What becomes clear here is that the metaphors we embrace about teachers, students, and schools will have an impact on our assessment praxis. Further, when we favor or assume certain metaphors of assessment, they often imply a certain view of teaching and learning. Before I describe my preferred metaphors of assessment, I will first discuss some that can be found in the educational literature.

Assessment as Measurement

Educators may think of learners, for instance, as blank slates, as trainable objects, as unfolding plants, as agents of social change, or as responsive image bearers of God. Each of these metaphors, as well as different metaphors for teaching and for curriculum, has implications not only for teaching and learning, but also for assessment. Far fewer educators explicitly create, accept, and use metaphors that allude directly to assessment—the subject of this chapter. Nevertheless, those that do so also portray a wide range of metaphors. Examples include assessment as measurement, as judgment, as inquiry, as incentive, as information generator, or as an art (Boud & Falchikov, 2006; Adelman, 1988; Delandshere, 2002; Fenwick and Parsons, 2009). Such metaphors fall into several categories that often overlap in practice: to highlight accountability and screening; to improve learning; to provide incentives for learning; and to give information about achievement.

First and foremost are metaphors that emphasize the role of assessment to establish accountability and data-based sorting of students. The most common metaphor describes assessment as measurement. Indeed, Hargreaves claims that the assessment as measurement metaphor has a "dominant influence in schools" and that "teachers sometimes believe it is the correct model, even if their own beliefs do not square with it" (2005, p. 222). She describes how the social efficiency model of the early twentieth century linked specific behavior and performance. She adds that this metaphor still dominates standardized testing throughout the world—and hence not only assessment but also the way we teach and learn.

There is little doubt that assessment is frequently equated with performance measurement, with counting beans, with hitting the mark, or with frequent and intense testing. The tests—often large-scale standardized ones—all too often measure what is easy to measure. They focus on verifying knowledge-that and knowledge-how of minor blips that fail to appraise the important goals of education such as higher-order thinking, problem posing and problem solving, and in-depth knowledge-why (Chudnovsky, 2006; Svidal, 2008). They use statistical measures of reliability and validity, ostensibly to demonstrate their scientific prowess. However, reliability just means that when two similar tests are given at different times expectations are that overall results will be similar. And validity is most commonly defined in terms of narrow learning outcomes that can easily be measured but that do not address the overall purpose of schooling.

A typical view is expressed by Peter Cowley, the creator of published ratings of all schools in British Columbia. He was quoted to say that "while it'd be great to measure qualities such as critical thinking and citizenship development, test scores are the only standardized data available province-wide" (Tebrake, 2009, p. A9). In other words, we neglect what cannot be counted, no matter how important, but count what does not count all that much—or, at least, count only a sliver of what schools ought to be about. And schools then begin to focus their curriculum and teaching more and more on that narrow slice that provincial or state exams assess. Even authors who emphasize that we should test what we value in terms of a school's mission may still assume that tests are a good measure of what students have learned. For example, Dan Vander Ark's book, *From Mission to Measurement,* has a chapter on "Teaching toward the Test" and ends his chapter on "Testing What You Value" with a further section on "Teach toward the Test" (Vander Ark, 2000).

Even when what we measure represents only a small part of what is important in education, the measurement metaphor assumes that assessment yields accountability. Educators who think of assessment as measurement thus speak of it as an audit of educational quality, as proof of learning achievement, and as a guarantee of educational quality. And those who believe in the soundness of such metaphors then take the next step and employ assessment as a screen to sort schools and students. In other words, they think of assessment as data-based decision making (Salvia & Ysseldyke, 2001), or as toll booths on a cross-country trip (Ladson-Billings, 2005). Assessment is seen as a well-crafted machine that legitimizes the ranking of schools and students (Rau, Shelley, & Beck, 2001). Little wonder, then, that the edition of the major newspaper in our area that sells the most copies each year is the one that ranks all elementary schools based on government standardized test results.

Treating assessment as measurement has one benefit: it makes us aware that learning should strive for certain standards. While those standards are often narrowly defined, measurement has led to improved specific literacy and numeracy skills. However, its results are also often used in simplistic and unfair judgmental ways, resulting in student indifference, despondency, and cynicism. Too often teachers are viewed as test administrators and students as objects to be manipulated to do well on tests. As such, assessment as measurement cannot avoid becoming assessment as judgment—judgment of schools, of teachers, and of students.

Assessment as Inquiry, as Incentive and as a Piano Lesson

Many educators are openly critical of viewing assessment as measurement, and decry its prevalence. They do not accept that assessment is an "objective" measurement process used for comparisons, judgments, and "treatments." They call for a paradigm shift. They agree with Vygotsky (1998) when he said, "We must not measure the child; we must interpret the child" (p. 204). They propose that assessment should be viewed as inquiry, inquiry that becomes a bridge to optimal learning (Delandshere, 2002). For them, assessment must scaffold learning. Curriculum and assessment, they hold, are the reverse sides of the coin of learning (Shoemaker & Lewin, 1993). Learning and assessment need to be in continuous dialogue. As Maddelena Taras (2008) put it, "Between teaching and learning assessment is the road. Not the hurdle." Frank Safarini similarly writes that assessment "is a process of inquiry, and a process of interpretation, used to promote reflection concerning students' understandings, attitudes, and literate abilities" (2000, p. 387). These educators see assessment as an integral part of learning, with both teachers and students examining, reflecting, diagnosing, discovering—and interacting about learning. Indeed, some go one step further and claim that we should view assessment *as* learning, with students being intimately involved in assessing their own learning and learning to take control of their own learning (Earl, 2003; Hargreaves, 2005).

Seeing assessment as inquiry leads both teachers and students to probe the results of both teaching and learning, and how learning can be enhanced. The focus of assessment is on observing and analyzing how learning takes place and can move forward, rather than on measurements that compare and rank, or that check whether specific targets have been attained. Considering assessment as inquiry has been shown to lead to improved learning if it involves meaningful formative feedback as well as student self-reflection and self-assessment of learning *for* learning. It sees teachers and students as responsible, interdependent persons, with the teacher taking the role of mentor, coach, and encourager. At the same time, proponents of this metaphor often hold that what is important is that students construct their own knowledge and meaning, often without recognizing or focusing on agreed-upon standards that students need to meet in order to function well in society.

In schools, educators tend to lean more toward either the assessment as measurement or the assessment as inquiry for learning metaphor. However, there are other, less common metaphors. For instance, some see assessment as incentive, as a carrot and a stick (Astin, 1991). Grades are used as rewards and punishment. The hope is that low grades for substandard work will motivate students to avoid failure. Government officials may use test results as a club to make schools and teachers "more responsible." Or parents may bribe students with a reward for getting good grades. Grades are held up as good indicators of how successful students will be in their careers. Note, however, that this metaphor is based on claims that research does not support.

Finally, many educators situate themselves somewhere between the measurement and inquiry metaphors. They see assessment as a generator of information, or as a procedure that provides data about learning that helps to establish a school's or school system's accountability, as well as to provide feedback that can lead to improved learning. Many do embrace both the measurement and the inquiry metaphors. In my jurisdiction, the government in its curriculum guides emphasizes assessment *for* learning and assessment *as* learning. The emphasis for both of these is on teacher and student reflection and evaluation that will lead to improved and further learning. But, at the same time, the government's Foundation Skills Assessment tests emphasize achievement in fairly narrow literacy and numeracy skills. By default, in the minds of parents—and also many school administrators—this summative measurement ends up taking on far more importance than the formative assessment that takes place in the classroom. Nevertheless, many teachers will emphasize supportive formative assessment in their classroom even though they recognize the potential though limited value of measurement through tests.

In this regard an intriguing metaphor is Alexander Astin's assessment as a piano lesson. Astin says that piano lessons, like assessment, should be rewarding and pleasurable for the student, with both teacher and student being interested in improvement. The assessment of success in the piano lesson is based on the outcome (accuracy, tempo, dynamics, etc.) as well as the process (how students hold their hands, how they practice, etc.). The information that the teacher acquires through performance analysis leads to relevant feedback that facilitates student learning and playing ability. The initial feedback leads to another performance, and further feedback as well as student reflection. While the emphasis is on cyclical feedback and performance, the teacher also informs the student regularly about her accomplishments in terms of certain criteria. In other words, Astin wants student assessment in the classroom to emphasize formative and supportive feedback to facilitate learning, but also wants teachers to inform students of the extent to which they have and have not met generally accepted criteria for success (Astin, 1991). And at some point the piano teacher will determine that a student has progressed as far as she is likely to go with a piece of music, and will give her a summative assessment.

Considering assessment as a generator of information can be useful for maintaining standards, diagnosing learning hurdles, and showing where instruction needs to be improved. However, this metaphor as well as the others I have discussed thus far fails to address sufficiently for what kind of society we are striving. How can our assessment metaphor and subsequent strategies help our graduates become active and contributing participants in such a society? To what end do we educate? What ought we to value? How can assessment promote justice rather than judgment in terms of what is important for life? How can it encourage the type of learning that allows our students to take on their roles in society in responsive and responsible ways?

In this regard, I believe that it is helpful to consider some metaphors that arise within the Judeo-Christian spiritual tradition.[2] In particular, I will consider, in turn, the implications of looking at assessment as a blessing, as grace, as justice, and, finally, as a covenant.

---

2. When I made a presentation about spiritual metaphors for assessment to a university faculty audience with a wide variety of religious and areligious views, a comment was made that I should also consider metaphors embedded in other religious traditions. While there may well be suitable metaphors in such traditions, I have not done so in this chapter. I myself am a Christian but am not sufficiently knowledgeable about other religions to do them justice. I do not feel qualified, for instance, to draw parallels between the four noble truths of Buddhism or the five pillars of Islam and student assessment in the classroom. I encourage persons within those or other religions to explore relevant metaphors that arise in their traditions.

Assessment as a Blessing

Student assessment should first of all encourage students to become more responsive in and responsible for their learning. It needs to contribute to students' acquiring meaningful knowledge-that, knowledge-how, and knowledge-why, leading them to gain insight and wisdom. Even the reporting of assessment results to parents and authorities must be done in ways that keep in mind that assessment aims to improve learning and achievement. Assessment must "enable students to unfold their gifts, to share the burdens of difficulties in learning, and to celebrate the joys of accomplishments" (Stronks and Blomberg, 1994, p. 275). In short, authentic assessment, to use a common phrase, is assessment that is a *blessing*, first of all for students, but also for teachers and parents.

Thinking of assessment as a blessing rather than as judgment or measurement involves a paradigm shift. Just think of the consequences of this metaphor. A blessing is a sign of favor that leads to well-being and productivity. Assessment as a blessing then serves as a way to support rather than to test students and their learning. Students will sense that teachers use assessment to work *with* them. They see that teachers will help them to develop and apply concepts, insights, abilities, and creative gifts, ones that enable them to make positive contributions to life in society. Assessment enables. It offers growth. It is a blessing, a gift[3] that leads to new and deeper learning.

John Trent and Gary Smalley describe how, in the Jewish and Christian Bible, bestowing the gift included five elements: a meaningful touch; a spoken message; attaching high value to the one being blessed; picturing a special future for the one being blessed; and an active commitment to fulfill the blessing (Trent & Smalley, 2004). These five elements, when blended together, result in students being able to thrive and make unique contributions within and to the learning community.

If assessment is to be a blessing, teachers first provide students with a meaningful "touch"—which, in today's society, means that we communicate warmth, personal acceptance, and affirmation to our students. Students learn more effectively when they feel that teachers sincerely and caringly use assessment strategies to encourage and improve their

---

3. A blessing is a particular kind of gift. It was an article by Elaine Brouwer (2006) on assessment as a gift that prompted me to develop the metaphor of assessment as a blessing.

efforts. Further, a blessing involves teachers giving spoken messages to all students that they are genuinely accepted and worthy of support, and that they celebrate that their students are valuable and have redeeming qualities. Teachers need to talk with each of their students regularly about their progress, both actual and perceived. They give feedback, and they correct in loving, helpful, and patient ways, in a context of supportive but persistent and well-planned instruction. As they assess they verbally recognize accomplishments and challenge students to further learning and growth. Sometimes the spoken message may be "tough love"—truth that is not pleasant, but spoken in love and with encouragement.

Through teachers' spoken messages students realize that their learning is valued and that teachers do their best to assess learning carefully and fairly, in ways that will lead to improvement. Assessment strategies that demonstrate students' worth include helping them recognize and confidently develop their gifts. I remember a weak math student who wanted to participate in a national mathematics contest. I encouraged her and gave her extra help to prepare even though we both knew (and discussed) that her final score would not be high. The fact that she was allowed to participate as well as her assessed placement (nationally at about the 25th percentile among students who were generally top math students) were both a blessing to her: she accomplished something she never thought possible. And I could praise her for her diligence and perseverance, two qualities that, I added, would stand her in good stead later in life (besides the fact that the extra work helped her in her regular math course). I also remember when as a high school staff we chose a valedictorian who academically barely passed her courses. We picked her because her gifts of compassion for others, her involvement in community service, and her personal positive influence on the class and school atmosphere made her, in our assessment, the outstanding student of the year. Our choice spoke volumes. We blessed her and blessed the other students by assessing and openly recognizing her valuable impact on the school.

A blessing, according to Trent and Smalley, also pictures a special future for the person being blessed. That means that our evaluation of assessment data must hold before our students the possibilities of what they can do with their special gifts. Those prospects may not be what students have dreamt of. Nor can we predict students' futures accurately. However, assessment can lead us to help students set meaningful goals based on their strengths. A former student of mine, now a senior pastor of a large church, shared with me an experience in high school that I had long forgotten but that had affected him a great deal. I had made a written comment on a math test on which he got an "A-." My comment was that he needed to start using his abilities more effectively. I said he was just marking time, and should turn his life around—and he did as a result of our discussion. My assessment held before him a picture of what was possible in his life, and in that way the assessment (in a subject he seldom used after high school!) became a blessing for him.

Finally, a blessing entails an active commitment. Words alone cannot communicate the blessing. Teachers need to back assessment with a commitment to do everything possible to help students to be successful. They provide the tools. They make available suitable space and time. They provide second and third chances. They provide extra help for students who need it. They hold them responsible, at the same time, for their efforts at improvement. They remain actively committed to their students with insight and staying power, and hold before them the need for them to be committed to their calling as students. Teachers become students of their students in order to grasp how their assessment can genuinely bless them.

Trent and Smalley describe the Orthodox Jewish custom that bestows weekly blessings on each child, stating that this "is considered an important vehicle for communicating a sense of identity, meaning, love, and acceptance" (Trent and Smalley, 2004, p. 39). The time of blessing often includes concrete signs that affirm the unique worth of the child: a special meal, laying on of hands, a word picture to praise the child, or a request to God to provide a special future for the child. Our assessment procedures and actions similarly ought to provide tangible evidence to our students that they have worth as individuals, that we appreciate genuine effort, that we want to help them use their strengths and overcome or deal with their limitation, and that they can achieve a special calling where they can make the most of their gifts. A friend told me recently that his mathematics teacher in high school had time and again told him that "he wouldn't amount to much." My friend is both determined and bright. He set out to prove the teacher wrong, and turn what he considered a curse into a blessing. He is now a successful orthopedic surgeon. However, most students would have been disheartened by such a continuous verdict. When assessments turn out to be a judgmental curse rather than a supportive blessing, most students become indifferent to and even hopeless about learning. They learn to feel rejected, to expect failure, and to be incompetent. Instead, our assessments need to bless students if they are to realize their potential.

Assessment as Grace

Donovan Graham points out that "in no other dimension of school life is it more difficult to put grace into practice than [student] evaluation" (2003, p. 256). In the Christian tradition, he continues, God evaluates our actions, but God has infinite patience with us and in his grace always gives us another chance to try again. He accepts us in weak as well as in strong performance. Similarly, teachers can use assessment of student work that includes failure or has room for improvement to produce eventual success and thus use it as a means of grace. That implies that students who do not do well at a task ought to be given several opportunities to improve, with appropriate help from the teacher or others. It also means that teachers try to determine the reasons why work is less than acceptable, and, if possible, address the underlying causes.

According to Graham, that does not mean, however, that we do not maintain standards for learning. He points out that the biblical authors record that Jesus "did not hesitate in evaluating the work and attitudes of both His disciples and His enemies . . . So we need not avoid the evaluation of our students' outward work or of their inner attitudes" (Graham, 2003, p. 256). Graham's point is that teachers can maintain standards and at the same time use assessment as a means of grace. They do so if they affirm their students unconditionally as human beings, no matter what their academic success or their grades. At the same time, they help them turn bad into good and mistakes into successes. Then students can steadily come closer to meeting the intended learning outcomes.

What does that mean for assessment strategies? Teachers clarify the criteria for assessment at the start of an assignment, so that students are not ambushed. They make self- and peer-assessment a continuous and integral part of the learning process. They accept student failure and disappointment, painful though it may be, as a step to eventual success. Their observations lead to constructive help. They give students ample opportunity to demonstrate their learning achievements, time and again. They emphasize formative assessment, assigning grades only at the end of the assessment process. Moreover, they recognize grades as imperfect and not-always valid or reliable summaries of complex learning achieve-ments—and certainly not a measure of a student's worth as a person. Finally, they are willing to reconsider their assessments to ensure that evaluations are both fair and supportive of further learning. Teachers will not be able to overcome completely students' perception that letter grades indicate their worth as persons. But they can try to minimize that notion. They can discuss with their students how all of them are creatures with special abilities, special personalities, and special responsibilities—and what that means with respect to treating them with both grace and justice.

Assessment as Justice

Assessment as a blessing and assessment as grace do not encompass the whole scope of assessment, however. There does come a point where, for whatever reason, we may have to tell a student that he or she did not make the grade. After a considerable formative process, we do need to evaluate the extent to which students have progressed, and make decisions about their ability to move forward. Now telling students this can still be a bless-ing or a sign of grace, even when the evaluation is not all that positive. Students may see, for instance, that they did not put forth the effort of which they were capable and change their ways. Or they may begin to realize in what areas they can better use their gifts.

The key question here is whether we have made such a judgment fairly. Has the decision been reached impartially and justly on the ba-sis of clear criteria? Have we applied our assessment as *justice*? In the Bible, the same word denotes justice and righteousness. The prophets in particular insist on right action and fair dealing, within a framework of grace: "Let justice roll on like a river, righteousness like a never-failing stream!" (Amos 5:24). Justice, not knowledge of or adherence to insig-nificant details, is to be the measuring line (Isaiah 28). Justice in the sense of fairness, righteousness, evenhandedness, and integrity needs to be the hallmark of both formative and summative assessment. Judgment in the sense of a critical final verdict is more appropriate in the courtroom than in the classroom.

Teachers who consider assessment as justice try to treat all students justly and fairly. They assess students on the basis of clearly defined crite-ria. They avoid pre-judgments on the basis of previous performance. They do not penalize students for taking risks. Their formative comments are fair and constructive. Whenever possible, they do not "count" first efforts for final grades. Their test content represents a fair sampling of the important learning outcomes, and provides different questions for students with different strengths. They are willing to explain why they reach certain conclusions, and admit when they have made assessment slip-ups. Their grading procedures are linked to stated learning outcomes. Their grades are a fair reflection of students' most recent performance. So their assessments help students develop and exercise their diverse abilities in optimal ways. Unless we evaluate the results in terms of students' abilities, we discourage them in their call to be wise stewards of their gifts. So we should praise the person who doubles his "one talent" as much as the one who doubles her "five talents." Moreover, if a student has only one talent, say, in mathematics, we should do whatever we can to ensure that he or she can function in life with basic mathematics skills. But we should also find other areas where such students can develop and apply their abilities in notable and joyful ways. At the same time, we must avoid prematurely reaching conclusions about particular weaknesses.

Assessment as justice can be difficult to achieve. That is particularly true when teachers assign summative grades. John Van Dyk describes what he calls "the agony of grading": "Grading raises feelings of jealousy. It introduces questions of fairness when two students have made all of the required effort but one wins and another loses because of difference in giftedness and circumstances. Grading creates adversarial relationships between students and teacher when students do not see evenhandedness in what in any case remains a subjective judgment" (2007, p. 155). Nor are these the only problems with grades. A "B" assigned by two teachers does not mean the same thing, which raises inter-class issues of justice. But two "Bs" assigned by the same teacher for two students in the same class and subject may also mean very different things. In one case it may mean that the student has conscientiously memorized and replicated information, but struggles to address issues with higher order thinking. For the other student, however, it may mean that he is insightful and creative but that as a procrastinator his work was sporadic throughout the unit. So is it fair to assign a "B" to both students? From the point of giving accurate information about achievement in terms of ability, no. Yet society demands that grades be given. The way to be as just as possible is, I believe, to emphasize formative assessment without assigning grades, and then to accompany grades with comments that provide a perspective on achievement in terms specific abilities, effort, attitude, participation, self-directedness, and so on.

Educators are part of a system that puts constraints on them. But if they look at assessment as a blessing for students and as extending grace to them, then they will also attempt to be as fair and as just as they can be as they assess students in order to support and encourage learning.

Conclusion: Assessment as Covenant

The key question for assessing students is how we can manage assessment practices for the benefit of students while at the same time showing parents and others that graduates have attained the vision and aims of the school. In this connection Wiggins and McTighe (2005) make the point that it is good practice for teachers to determine what evidence they need to assess whether learning goals have been achieved, and then to develop appropriate assessment strategies before planning student learning experiences. Certainly it is important to carefully plan assessment procedures prior to teaching a topic or unit. And such strategies will include formative teacher- peer- and self-assessment as well as some measurement of understanding and skills. However, if the assessment is to extend blessing, grace, and justice to students, formative inquiry about learning as well as measurement will do so in order to help students attain pre-determined learning outcomes and standards that are clear and comprehensive consequences of the mission of a school. Such assessment includes assessment of knowledge, of understandings, of abilities, of dispositions and attitudes, and of commitment to values. And while some comparisons cannot be avoided, the intent of measurement should be to help students see to what degree they have achieved specified outcomes, and how they can best make further progress.

What is clear is that when teachers focus on formative assessment *for* and *as* learning, rather than on summative assessment *of* learning, student learning makes considerable gains—and assessment becomes more of a blessing to students. Dylan Wiliam (2006) describes some key strategies to make this a reality. On the basis of his assessment of how assessment helps learning, he recommends teachers to clarify intended learning outcomes and achievement criteria with learners. They should provide feedback that moves students ahead. Also, they should implement discussions, activities, and tasks that bring out evidence of learning outcome attainment. Moreover, they ought to have students take ownership of their learning through assessing their own work and frequently reflect on their goals, strategies, and outcomes. Finally, they should coach students to support each other in their learning tasks. And when teachers use summative assessment, they must also use it to enable students to learn, both during and as a result of the assessment. Elsewhere I describe more strategies for implementing assessment as a blessing, as grace and as justice, as well as a sample school assessment policy.[4]

However, to change the assessment model from one of teachers calculating and transmitting scores and grades to one where assessment becomes a collaborative inquiry-based (ad)venture will require a change of mindsets. Such a paradigm shift will not come about easily. It will take time, re-evaluation of current practices, dialogue with colleagues, opportunities to try new strategies, and leadership support. Lack of time may well be the largest hurdle. Large class sizes as well as little time for preparation and professional development often stand in the way of giving meaningful personal feedback and implementing desirable change. However, teachers can make two or three adjustments in their assessment strategies each year, even if they are small ones, in order to move toward assessment becoming a blessing for their students.

The biblical concept of covenant is helpful in summing up what I believe about assessment. Strictly speaking, a covenant is a binding agreement or compact between two parties with both benefits and obligations on both sides. But the Bible recounts God's making covenants at his initiative, with no evident benefits to himself, and promises that he will bless those who are part of his covenant. He emphasizes a continuing fruitful relationship that is the heart of the covenant: "I will be your God, and you will be my people" (Leviticus 26:12). If the people follow God's decrees, that is, if they reciprocate to God's covenant, he pledges plentiful harvests and peace in the land. If they do not, if they are unfaithful, the consequences will be the loss of blessing. Yet time and again God also extends grace to those who fail to respond to him in kind, and even to those who reject him, once they demonstrate a willingness to return to God's leading and guidance.

4. See Van Brummelen (2009), Chapter 5.

What does this have to do with assessment? Let me assure you that I do not want to consider teachers as gods in their classrooms! However, teachers have been given authority in order to serve and equip their students, and students have a calling to exercise their gifts. As such, teachers and students stand in a covenantal relationship. And student assessment is part of that covenantal bond. Teachers pledge to do what is best for their students and their learning through their instruction, their mentoring—and their assessment of learning. The key to "covenantal" assessment is that when teachers and students abide by the covenant, assessment will bless both: students are blessed by gaining insights and skills as a result of the assessment; the teachers' vocation becomes more rewarding in seeing students make good progress within a supportive learning community. Teachers also extend grace when students fall short, and help and encourage them to succeed a next time. And teachers are just. If students fulfill their calling, the teachers' assessments will indicate that they have employed their gifts well in terms of the gifts they have. At the same time, if students do not hold up their side of the covenant relationship (e.g., they time and again fail to live up to their responsibilities), then teachers will face them with consequences because they have broken the trust of a covenantal relationship.

Assessment as covenant. It is an ideal, one that perhaps we never reach. Teachers fall short; students founder; classes have dynamics that sometimes undermine a teacher's best efforts. Yet I am convinced that conceiving of assessment as a covenantal relationship that brings about blessing, grace, and justice will yield dividends in the lives of both students and teachers. Let our assessment do more than focus on hitting the mark: let it light the candle of learning and thus enlighten the lives of our students.

References

Adelman, C. (Ed.). (1988). *Performance and judgment: Essays on principles and practice in the assessment of college student learning.* ERIC document ED 299 888. Washington, DC: Office of Educational Research and Improvement.

Astin, A. (1991). *Assessment for excellence: The philosophy and practice of assessment and evaluation in higher education.* Santa Barbara, CA: Greenwood Publishing Group.

Boud, D. & Falchikov, N. (2006). Aligning assessment with long-term learning. *Assessment & Evaluation in Higher Education 31*(4), 399–413.

Brouwer, E. (2006). Assessment as gift: A vision. In E. Brouwer & R. Koole (Eds.), *Educating toward wisdom* (pp. 2.1–2.2). Langley, BC: Society of Christian Schools in British Columbia.

Chudnovsky, D. (2006). Authentic assessment of students. *Our Schools, Our Selves 16*(1), 29–32.

Dantley, M. (2003). Purpose-driven leadership: The spiritual imperative to guiding schools beyond high-stakes testing and minimum proficiency. *Education and Urban Society 35*(3), 273–291.

Deakin Crick, R. (2007). Learning how to learn: The dynamic assessment of learning power. *The Curriculum Journal 18*(2), 135–153.

Delandshere, G. (2002). Assessment as inquiry. *Teachers College Record 104*(7), 1461–1484.

Earl, L. (2003). *Assessment as learning: Using classroom assessment to maximize student learning*. Thousand Oaks, CA: Corwin Press.

Fenwick. T. & Parsons, J. (2009). *The art of evaluation: A resource for educators and trainers* (2nd ed.). Toronto, ON: Thompson Educational Publishers.

Graham, D. (2003). *Teaching redemptively: Bringing grace and truth into your classroom*. Colorado Springs, CO: Purposeful Design Publications.

Hargreaves, E. (2005). Assessment for learning? Thinking outside the (black) box. *Cambridge Journal of Education 35*(2), 213–224.

Ladson-Billings, G. (2005). Crossing over to the Jordan: The journey of new teachers in diverse classrooms. *Education and Urban Society 37*(3), 356–360.

McKillop, C. (2006). Drawing on assessment: Using visual representations to understand students' experiences of assessment in art and design. *Art, Design & Communication in Higher Education 5*(2), 131–144.

Ormell, C. (1996). Eight metaphors of education. *Educational Research 38*(1), 67–75.

Rau, W., Shelley, M., & Beck, F. (2001). The dark engine of Illinois education: A sociological critique of a "well-crafted (testing) machine. *Educational Policy 15*(3), 404–431.

Safarini, F. (2000). Three paradigms of assessment: Measurement, procedure, and inquiry. *The Reading Teacher 54*(4), 385–393.

Salvia, J. & Ysseldyke, J. (2001). *Assessment* (8th ed.). Boston: Houghton Mifflin.

Shoemaker, B. & Lewin, L. (1993). Curriculum and assessment: Two sides of the same coin. *Educational Leadership 51*(8), 55–57.

Stronks, G. & Blomberg, D. (1993). *A vision with a task: Christian schooling for responsive discipleship*. Grand Rapids, MI: Baker.

Svidal, S. (2008). Reframing education. *ATA News 43*(8), 6.

Taras, M. (2008). Between teaching and learning, assessment is the road, not the hurdle. Address at the European Educational Research Association, 2008 Annual Conference, September 10, 2008, Göteborg, Sweden.

Tebrake, R. (2009). John Oliver a report-card success story. *The Vancouver Sun*, June 17, 2009, A9.

Theobald, D. (2009). Our schools are our gardens. *Alberta Teachers Association News 43*(13), 2.

Trent, J. & Smalley, G. (2004). *The blessing: Giving the gift of unconditional love and acceptance* (Revised and Repacked Ed.). Nashville, TN: Thomas Nelson.

Tuttle, H. (2009). Frequent formative assessment: Road trip metaphor. *Education with technology Harry G. Tuttle* website. Retrieved from http://eduwithtechn.wordpress.com/2009/05/16/frequent-formative-assessment-road-trip-metaphor/

Van Brummelen, H. (2009). Walking with God in the classroom: Christian approaches to teaching and learning (3rd Ed.). Colorado Springs, CO: Purposeful Design Publications.

Vander Ark, D. (2000). *From mission to measurement*. Grand Rapids, MI: Christian Schools International.

Van Dyk. J. (2007). *Fostering a reflective culture in the Christian school: The Maplewood story*. Sioux Center, IA: Dordt College Press.

Vygotsky, L. (1998). The problem of age. In R. Rieber (Ed.), *Collected works of L. S. Vygotsky*. New York: Plenum. (Vol. 5, pp. 187–205). New York: Kluwer Academic/ Plenum Publishers.

Wiggins, G. & McTighe, J. (2005). *Understanding by Design* (2nd Ed.). Alexandria, VA: Association for Supervision and Curriculum Development.

Wiliam, D. (2006). Assessment for learning: Why, what, and how? *Orbit 36*(2), 2–6.

seven

Princesses and Superheroes: Metaphors that Work Against Wholeness

Allyson Jule

Every girl can be a princess.
Any dream can be; close your eyes and see.
A magic wand and soon you're gone
from just you to royalty.

—DISNEY'S EVERY GIRL CAN BE A PRINCESS

Ninja Turtles are on the scene
You mess with green and it's gonna get mean
Ninja Turtles are on the scene
You mess with green and it's gonna get mean

—TEENAGE MUTANT NINJA TURTLES SONG

IN 2000, DISNEY CORPORATION began grouping several of its female movie characters together as "Disney Princesses" (Snow White, Sleeping Beauty, Cinderella, Ariel, Belle, Jasmine, Mulan and Pocahontas). Since then, the Disney princess business has grown from $300 million that first year to $4 billion internationally in 2008. Clearly, this constitutes a brilliant marketing move that targets a normal stage of child development and exploits the vulnerability and attraction to larger-than-life personas (Orenstein, 2006). By age three, children are beginning to define themselves and others as gendered. They are also at a height of imaginative play. For boys, this often manifests itself in strong superheroes, while girls are socialized into more passive roles (Gallas, 1998). However, the more recent princess phenomenon has become more ubiquitous because it sets young girls on a higher and small pedestal, while the superhero version for boys sets up a demand for physical domination and power.

Both parents of young children and primary teachers recognize the power of metaphors in play. The princess is a key focus in girls' fantasy life, and many boys are drawn to the images of superheroes; children use such metaphors as characters in their fantasy lives. There is great appeal to fantasy play and it is an important developmental stage of forming imagination in the important stage of play-as-learning. Children play out what they see in the world around them and imagine themselves in alternative worlds. There is power in childhood metaphors to deeply influence the emotional development of young children and influence their future ambitions and attitudes. As such, this chapter suggest that the "princess" and the "superhero" metaphors may work to encourage a capitalist agenda of need rather than a more fully developed selfhood and greater personal wholeness that could be found in less gender-stereotyping ways. The *imago Dei* for Christian primary educators offers a critical alternative.

The Princess and the Superhero

A princess needs to accomplish very little other than to be beautiful—in sharp contrast to a queen who might actually have some power and maturity. The princess serves as a metaphor of passive and objectified femininity. She is the ultimate young woman because of her given rather than earned status: her special innate beauty. Intelligence and competence are not requirements for the role of princess. The superhero is action-based, perhaps violent, even when doing good deeds. The superhero is task-driven and accomplishes things, like saving the world. In this way, the superhero for boys serves as metaphor of active masculinity. Both of these pervasive gendered metaphors give children critical messages about gender roles very early in their childhood. Davies (2003) says, "Childhood, it would appear, is a privileged time as far as the fantasy world is concerned, since children are quite deliberately presented with models of the world that are, at least on the surface of things, entirely fanciful. But the moral order is deeply embedded in that fanciful world. The division of the world into 'real' and 'fantasy' is itself an essential key to the establishment" (p.

45). The princess fairy tale is a persistent one for many young girls in Western culture. Images of pink dresses and silver tiaras are found everywhere: in movies, at toy stores, in books, at girls' birthday parties and as popular Halloween costumes. It is a persuasive ideal promoted by books as well as bedroom decor. The princess metaphor is celebrated by all things pink, frilly, and sparkly. Princess castles seem to be ubiquitous in playrooms, daycare centers and primary classrooms. Princess Barbie and Princess Bratz dolls are popular gift ideas and princess accessories are easy to find in stores. The princess message begins practically at birth with everything from princess baby shirts and bibs to pink picture frames for baby girls. By the time girls are toddlers, many are drawn to princess dresses, glittery crowns and princess make-up, stickers, and attitudes.

Superheroes are also marketed aggressively, though I believe the male gender stereotype is less damaging than what is offered to girls in the princess world. Boys are presented with images of male role models who are active, powerful, and effective. Boys play together and reach for a strong, independent selfhood. They can enjoy being "one of the boys"; they use toy guns and act aggressively but together. Just as we give girls princess playthings, we give boys superhero toys and accessories. Many stories geared to boys use the superhero as the main character, and movies with superheroes are marketed to young boys. Young boys dress up as their favorite superhero and embody the character's actions, attitudes and motivations. The masculinity presented in superhero play is a hyper-macho one where achievement is based on physical strength, assertiveness, and power. Courage is a positive aspect, one that the girls are rarely presented with in the princess metaphor. Davies (2003) states "To 'be a man' is to show the qualities needed to sustain power—courage in the face of threat or conflict—qualities that define an admired, socially dominant form of masculinity. But this does not settle the everyday reality of men's lives, for most men can't or won't live according to this 'ideal' pattern. Rather, it defines a basic *tension* in masculinity" (p. 129). Other attributes, such as intelligence or compassion or concern for others, are only valuable when supportive of the powerful main character. The superhero glory comes from victory over others.

For well over fifty years, six year old girls as princesses and boys as superheroes have been staples of childhood play. What is so different now? My worry about these pervasive metaphors, particularly the princess metaphor for young girls, is due in part to the assumptions of extravagance and entitlement that feed a growing industry that is based exclusively on an impossible fantasy world that is vapid, emotionally stunted, and ultimately powerless. A seemingly harmless rite of passage may well have problematic long-term effects on gender identity and on one's sense of worth in the world. The princess metaphor for "pretty" and "glamorous" attracts young girls to an unrealistic fairy tale and sets them up for a reality of disappointment and/or superficiality While the metaphor for "power" and "strength" attracts young boys to an unrealistic alternative life, though I believe the superhero metaphor is not as problematic for boys as the princess one is for young girls. "Some forms of 'masculinity' and 'femininity' are 'safe.' If correctly achieved, they are recognized as high-status ways of being. The children who achieve them are popular and other children aspire to be in their group. The superhero boys, the 'home corner' girls, the rough, tough princesses and the sirens have adopted the major 'safe' forms. These forms fall clearly within the poles of gender and do not overlap or undermine the sense of oppositeness" (Davies, 2003, p.131).

While both metaphors have the potential to undermine a fuller exploration of gender identity and expectations in young girls and boys, the more sustainable attribute of action makes the superhero more affirming of personal agency. Regardless, these messages of simplistic and assumed gendered performances need not be reinforced in the primary classroom. Primary teachers, and Christian teachers in particular, should use alternative and varied metaphors for femininity and masculinity in choosing books and stories and in learning activities for their classrooms. I believe it is imperative to present a wider range of choice and alternative metaphors for play and to set the image-bearers of God as a better metaphor to selfhood.

Princess Parenting and Superhero Teaching

Regretfully, these metaphors limit possibilities of gender ambiguity or alternative explorations that might allow for more authenticity. Societal support for princess play and "princess parenting" leads to a kind of supports the princess play as "princess parenting". This leads to a kind of breeding of narcissism that is not modeled the same way in boys. Twenge and Campbell (2009) explored the growing rate of college-age women who grew up with the princess metaphor surrounding them as a marketing reality, and they suggest that young women are developing narcissistic traits four times that of college-age men. They also point out that today's college-age women were young girls when some of the newer and most popular Disney princess films were released and marketed as toys, posters, clothes, etc. In response, Disney has recently released a line of princess-inspired prom and wedding dresses aimed at this group of women, promoting a "diva habit" that is celebrated by mothers and girls of all ages.

Boyd (1997) recognizes the growing concern over superhero play in her research, citing the doubling of research studies on the subject from 1990 to 1995. She reviews the concerns about such play in primary classrooms due to what is perceived as boys' inappropriate behavior by teachers concerning violence and hyper-active play. However, her own review of various studies on boys and superhero play in schools suggests that teachers may be over-reporting the occurrences and nature of superhero play, leading to an inflated estimate of this behavior. For example, children and teachers may have different views on what is play-fighting or aggression rather than superhero imaginative play. She focuses on several studies of boys' play where superhero play happens without play-fighting or aggression and where the play is highly collaborative and supportive.

Parsons and Howe (2006) researched the play dyads of preschool boys in various play sessions and compared superhero play and non-superhero play and found that boys were more (not less) aggressive and physically active in non-superhero play. In fact, Parsons and Howe suggest that superhero play is highly imaginative and that boys displayed more collaborative activity and language use in superhero play than boys not engaging in superhero play. Such possibilities cannot be overlooked, even though attitudes of entitlement may be similar and feed highly gendered expectations.

Christian teachers in particular can and perhaps should be powerful interrupters of these gendered metaphors. They should avoid being silent or being collaborators and encouragers of highly gendered play. Why support superficial and pop-culture worship inside their classrooms? The all-princess-all-the-time mindset surely prevents larger possibilities. Likewise, the superhero-at-all-costs mentality restrains the possibility of building supportive and loving communities. A total immersion into a violent fantasy world limits meaningful connections with a larger world, one that includes developing insight and learning to give way to others, whether that be through sports, museum, outdoor, reading, and other creative learning activities. Given the way that such immersion limits these wider connections, classroom stories and displays need to be sensitive to gender exclusivity and focus more purposefully on the shared intellectual, social, emotional, aesthetic, and physical worlds where a fuller exploration of learning and development can occur.

Princess and Superhero Aspirations

Disney movies and books have often featured male leads who seek adventure: *Peter Pan, Robin Hood* and *The Lion King*. Too often, when females do enter the picture, they are princesses or they aspire to be princesses or they are rewarded for their beauty by becoming princesses, such as *Sleeping Beauty, Beauty and the Beast* and *Cinderella*. The female characters are in relation to a male figure with the power to save them in some critical way. Her beauty is often his reward for courage and strength. Significantly, in the original *Sleeping Beauty* story the Prince happened upon Sleeping Beauty quite by chance: individual heroics was an emphasis added by Disney.

The *See Jane* organization, a media watch program, was founded by Oscar award winning actress Geena Davis in 2004. Its research has been carried out by Stacy Smith (2006a, 2006b) at the University of Southern California, Los Angeles, and has explored G-rated (G for General—family viewing) movies and the portrayal of female and male characters in films marketed to children. Smith and her team explored 101 top-grossing family-rated films released from 1990 through to 2004, analyzing a total of 4249 speaking characters in the movies, including both animated and live action films. Smith found that, overall, three out of four characters (75%) are male, while fewer than one in three (28%) speaking characters are female. Fewer than one in five (17%) characters in crowd scenes are female and more than four out of five (83%) film narrators are male. Smith (2006A) also found that G-rated movies show very few examples of parents as characters, let alone showing them as partners in a marriage or other committed relationship.

For all of us, but especially for children, images and stories help influence the important developmental task of understanding what it means to be human, whether male or female. In a 2003 American nationwide survey, the Kaiser Family Foundation found that half of all children aged zero to six watch at least one DVD movie per day. In view of this, G-rated movies no doubt have an influence on children's early social learning about gender roles because children also tend to watch the same movies over and over. Other studies explore the television viewing habits among children and suggest that gender expectations can become very simplified, skewed and stereotypical in nature (Herrett-Skjellum & Allen, 1996). Since women and girls make up half the human race, the *See Jane* media watch group believes the presence of a wider variety of female characters in children's earliest experiences with the media is essential for both girls' and boys' development. If both boys and girls see more female characters of all types, all of us may experience a fuller awareness of the possible ways to be human.

The *imago Dei*

From a Christian perspective, each person is an image-bearer of God, created in God's image—*imago Dei* (Genesis 1:27). In this way, "learning is meaningful only when it leads to an understanding of God's call" (Van Brummelen, 2009, p. 99). As Christian teachers, we see all students as in God's likeness. Humanity itself is created to reflect the Holy within human nature and we reveal *imago Dei* in all our best qualities. We are called to serve God and to be like God. What does this mean in the primary classroom? Christian teachers must see their students—all their students—as image-bearers. In this regard, the princess and the superhero work against a higher dignity of the human soul: there is more to being a person than being gendered.

As Andy Crouch (2008) has pointed out, it is significant that in an era when everything was written on scarce parchment, the author of Genesis repeated four times in just two verses that humans—both male and female—are created in God's image. In the chapters on God's work of creation, the author wanted to emphasize that humans were not only given the responsibility of caring for creation and unfolding its possibilities. Like God, they were to be creators. A such, they would be cultivators of culture. They had been endowed with abilities to re-make the world and contribute to the flourishing of human life. They were to be part of God's cosmic plan for societies and lives that could experience and celebrate *shalom*. But princesses live in Disney's pre-planned theme parks where they have to fit a predetermined and narrowly defined role. And superheroes live in fantasy worlds—often violent ones—that rule out building communities of vision, resourcefulness, humility, and grace. Neither the princess nor the superhero role can do justice to children being and becoming imaginative cultivators of their own lives and of their surroundings.

Teachers therefore are required to enable their students to be their best selves—including the development of God-like traits like creativity, insight, competence, care for others and for the world, mercy, justice and humility. In such ways, students need guidance, supervision and discipline and to direct "their students in the way [they] should go" (Proverbs 22:6). Entitlement and arrogance are not godly virtues and work against the *imago Dei*. When Christian teachers turn their attention to the "renewing" of minds (Romans 12:2), children can see a fuller human experience, one that is imaginative, capable, productive, compassionate, insightful, patient, loving, peace-making and godly. Such a focus makes teaching a far richer one than replicating gender stereotypes or reinforcing empty fantasy metaphors as "ideal." Christian teachers need to "choose content so that [they] encourage students to take up their intended calling as bearers of God's image" (Van Brummelen, 2009, p.103). Humanity is created in both the image and likeness of God. A personal wholeness requires guidance, protection, and modeling. The princess and the superhero do not model the finest of human qualities and, therefore, should not be the main guiding forces of childhood fantasy life.

Every Child a Person

Sexism is deeply rooted in the West's consumerist individualism. The market keeps generating products that support and encourage a huge demographic with disposable income. Even though most girls may grow out of a "princess phase," mainstream, middle-class, usually white Americans support such images of children because they are comfortable, recognizable, known, and superficially promise success for everyone. (See www.abcnews.go.com, 2007, for blog chat for parents.) The formula of men as bread-winners (and therefore heroes) and women as home-makers (and therefore the home's princess to be rescued and cared for) is one that is a dated stereotype but has nevertheless worked for millions of the middle class, including, and perhaps even especially, for the Christian sub-culture. But I think we must expect Christian teachers to better understand the power of media images and to seek out stories which present more fullness to human behavior and intentions. Thankfully, some movies for children have nothing to do with princesses or superheroes, such as *Chicken Run, Castle in the Sky, Lilo and Stitch, Alice in Wonderland* and *Monsters, Inc.* Christian teachers would be wise to focus on gender-neutral, gender-bending, or gender-healing stories, pointing toward the *imago Dei* as the model for behavior.

One popular alternative story is the Canadian classic children's book by Robert Munsch, *The Paper Bag Princess.* It was published to great critical acclaim in 1980, and it has since sold over three million copies worldwide. The story begins in a traditional enough way. Prince Ronald plans to marry the lovely Elizabeth. However, a dragon arrives who destroys Elizabeth's kingdom and all her princess clothing (leaving her with only a paper bag to wear) and takes Prince Ronald. It falls to the plucky Elizabeth to rescue her prince. She does this by tricking the dragon to fly around the world two times. This challenge exhausts him and he falls asleep. Elizabeth saves Ronald but, instead of thanking her, he tells her to "come back when you look like a real princess." Elizabeth tells him off, calling him a "bum," and doesn't marry him after all. This book reverses the princess and dragon stereotype. Using such stories in the primary classroom presents both girls and boys a more human, less simplified stereotypic view of being a person and, yes, it opens up a more authentic humanity, something Christian teachers should champion.

Another more recent children's book is *Princess Bubble* (2007). The story stars a princess who is confused by the fairy tale messages that say she must marry a prince before she can live happily ever after. Princess Bubble dons her "thinking crown" to research fairy tales and interviews her married princess friends. With help from her fairy godmother, Ms. Bubble discovers that living happily ever after is not about finding a prince. True happiness comes from being kind to others and being comfortable with one's self. *Oliver is a Sissy* is an alternative story regarding masculinity. Such stories can potentially open up discussion for less rigid and demanding gender roles.

Conclusion

The marketing overload in today's capitalist society is limiting choices about what it means to be a girl or a boy. Perhaps other versions of the princess or superhero can help offer alternative metaphors for children, offering other traits of value and meaning and self-worth. Other metaphors can and do exist. As Christian teachers, we want our students to know they are valued for deeper character traits other than how they look or what power they can use over others. In fact, such traits work against Christian virtues of mercy, justice and humility.

Both the princess and superhero metaphors are all about being special, about being the one who gets all the attention, but alternative models for being human must also be presented so that girls are not constantly fed the idea that their appearance is the only necessary trait or that boys are not constantly fed the idea that their power over others is the only vital characteristic available for them. It is important to present other models so that girls do not see boys as false superheroes and boys do not see girls as helpless princesses to be rescued and adored. When girls and boys focus on superficial gender roles, they cannot focus on the many other ways to be in their world and to contribute to society in deeper ways. The multi-million dollar industry is convincing girls that they must be pretty, special and magical to be worthwhile, and convincing boys that they must be strong, physically powerful and aggressive to be significant. Such a narrowly defined personhood that uses surface-level gender roles to engage the world of fantasy and reality limits a more well-rounded childhood. Christian teachers in particular must recognize the problems for both boys and girls embedded in such metaphors and find alternative stories, movies, and fantasy play props so to develop a fuller sense of self.

> So God created human beings in his own image.
> In the image of God he created them;
> male and female he created them.
>
> (GENESIS 1:27, NEW LIVING TRANSLATION)

References

Boyd, B. (1997). Teacher response to superhero play: To ban or not to ban? *Childhood Education, 74*(1), 23–28.

Crouch, A. (2008). *Culture making: Recovering our creative calling*. Downers Grove, IL: InterVarsity.

Davies, B. (2003). *Frogs and snails and feminist tales: Preschool children and gender*. Creskill, NJ: Hampton Press.

Disney Corporation. Every girl can be a princess. (2000). Los Angeles, CA: Disney.

Gallas, K. (1998*). "Sometimes I can be anything": Power, gender and identity in a primary classroom*. New York. Teachers College Press.

Johnson, S. & Tonelli, M. (2007). *Princess bubble*. Atlanta, GA: Bubble Gum Press.

Munsch, R. (1980). *The paper bag princess*. Toronto, ON: Anassi Press.

Orenstein, P. (2006). What's wrong with Cinderella? *New York Times* online, retrieved from http://www.nytimes.com/2006/12/24/magazine/24princess.t.html?pagewanted=all.

Parsons, A., & Howe, N. (2006). *Superhero toys and boys' physically active and imaginative play*. Olney, MD: Association for Childhood Education International.

Seerveld, C. (1988). *On being human: Imaging God in the modern world*. Burlington, ON: Welch Publishing.

Smith, S. L. (2006). *Where the girls aren't: Gender disparity saturates G-rated films*. Program Brief, See Jane. Retrieved from www.seejane.org

Twenge, J. & Campbell, W.K. (2009). *The narcissism epidemic: Living in the age of entitlement*. New York: Free Press.

Van Brummelen, H. (2009). *Walking with God in the classroom*. (3rd ed.) Colorado Springs, CO: Purposeful Design.

Vanderkam, L. (2009, August 12). The princess problem. *USA Today*. August 12, p. 92.

eight

Metaphors for Spirituality in Public Educational Settings

Monika B. Hilder

"WE CAN'T TALK ABOUT religion in public school." The year was 1970 and I was a grade 8 student in a public high school home economics classroom in Vancouver, British Columbia. I was Christian, my friend was Jewish, and we were comparing notes on our respective faiths. Our conversation was animated, respectful, highly interesting, but, as our teacher informed us, *verboten*. We submitted to being silenced. But to this day I still feel my slight twinge of embarrassment and greater flash of anger that students, apparently, had no public right to discuss what mattered most to us—how we viewed God, death, and the universe. Why could the educational powers muzzle free speech about who we thought we were as human beings? Those were in the very last days of Bible reading in monthly school assemblies before the high tide of secularism swept away such "dangerous anachronisms" with the incoming surge of increasing materialism and attending rationalistic reductionism.

The things that are forbidden can teach subversion, even perversion. We couldn't talk about religion? Of course we could. We did it all the time—in the hallways, in the classrooms out of teachers' earshot. Sometimes in an argumentative yet respectful way. Sometimes in a deeply personal, devotional way. Sometimes in a dismissive way. We were democratic, open-minded, and vocal critical thinkers—but not usually in the official learning space. Granted, in some literature classrooms we did discuss how authors viewed God: those classrooms were often some of the best places in which to engage spiritual questions. But when in biology our fine teacher cautioned, "Remember, evolution is just a theory," we understood that theories, like fashions, were temporary paradigms.

But somewhere in our public educational journey all of us (at least some of the time) engaged with, if not imbibed, the notion that the important things in academic achievement could and indeed should be separated from our religious worldviews, whether creedal, agnostic, or atheistic. In those shifting planes between the overt and the covert curriculum, we adolescents did not see clearly enough that all paradigms are constructs. Neither we nor perhaps our elders understood fully how worldviews inform our insights and, moreover, that the silencing of spirituality is indeed a paradigm that creates a dangerous vacuum. We did not quite realize that we were taught to dichotomize, essentially to lie.

The question of addressing spirituality, including its rootedness in various religions, in the public classroom is a thorny one. How does one do so in an educational, non-discriminatory, and non-proselytizing way? In a recent conversation with the director of an education press, I asked, "What comes to mind when you hear 'spirituality and education'?" He answered, "To be honest, the legal implications. How do you distinguish between religion and spirituality? And how do you do this in the public classroom?"

These questions have similar implications for creedal schools. The religious school educator who has the mandate and privilege to teach from a particular religious perspective needs to be equally and perhaps especially aware of his or her duty to honor each individual with genuine freedom of choice. Moreover, should not all educational enterprises ensure the sacred, inviolable right of each individual to explore and choose his and her own personal beliefs—without fear, without condemnation, and without coercion? But when we eliminate spirituality from the classroom, we lose this academic freedom, for the silencing of spirituality is another form of proselytization—a proselytization into a secularism that ignores historical, contemporary, and personal development.

This is neither ethical nor intelligent. How indeed does one behave like a historian without making reference to the major impact of religious thought on human history? How does one properly teach mathematics, asks Nel Noddings, without attentiveness to the philosophical and religious positions of its thinkers? (Noddings, 1993; Halford, 1998). How does one teach science without considering the various truth claims that have motivated its thinkers? How does one consider legal systems without reference to age-old philosophical positions? All these raise deeply spiritual and religious questions that are as old as humanity: Who am I? Is life meaningful? What values do I hold to and why? Katherine Paterson, citing the Chinese and Japanese ideographs for the word *idea* that combine the character for *sound* with the character for *heart,* puts it this way: "What are the sounds that I hear in my deepest heart? What causes me to shape human experience in the way that I do?" (1989, p. 45).

Twenty-first century responses to the question of spirituality in the classroom vary. In Canada, students are largely educated in a spiritual vacuum (Van Brummelen, Koole, & Franklin, 2004). Canadian author Douglas Coupland speaks of growing up with zero knowledge of Judeo-Christian thinking (Coupland, 1994; Levy, 2008). Yet other democratic countries like the United Kingdom stipulate that the exploration of spirituality be a curriculum goal. Throughout popular culture we notice the deepening interest in spirituality. How can educators approach this?

In this chapter I explore some metaphors that may help us address spirituality conscientiously in the public classroom in order to maximize freedom of thought and empowerment. Moreover, as a literature teacher, I will describe how these metaphors have been celebrated by authors with various spiritual sensibilities. I also give practical examples that address spirituality in ways that honor the sacred, inviolable right of individuals to develop as mature members of the planet. To do this, I first speak to the question, "What is spirituality?"

What is Spirituality?

The *Oxford English Dictionary* defines spirituality as "The quality or condition of being spiritual; attachment to or regard for things of the spirit as opposed to material or worldly interests." *Merriam-Webster's Dictionary* defines it as "gaining insight, knowledge and a better understanding about life." Mike Radford sees spirituality as referring "to those interrelated, non-material aspects of human development, the moral, personal, and maybe aesthetic dimensions, as well as some form of experience of the transcendent" (2003, p. 255). The sheer volume of publications on spirituality attests to its importance in popular as well as academic culture. The existence of a journal such as the *International Journal of Children's Spirituality,* for instance, demonstrates this point. In the realm of public education, the debate ranges from opposition (Blake, 1996; Marples, 2005) to affirmation (Anderson, 2004; Carr, 1995 & 1996; Huebner, 1985 & 1993; Palmer, 1983, 1998/1999; Noddings, 1993; and Smith, 2000).

Early in the twentieth century, Alfred North Whitehead wrote, "the essence of education is that it be religious" (1929, p. 14). He challenged the traditional American understanding of the separation of church and state. His view that spirituality—seen more broadly than formal religion—ought to be present in education has been echoed by many later curriculum thinkers. Dwayne Huebner spoke of education as "the lure of the transcendent" (1985, p. 360) and insisted that "the ultimate goal of education [was] the journey of the soul" (1993, p. 406). William F. Pinar et al. (1995/2000) identified "theological text" as a curriculum orientation. Nel Noddings spoke of the ethical necessity of educating all students for intelligent belief or disbelief (Noddings, 1993; Halford, 1998/99). Students need to know, she argued, what faith and non-faith positions inform thinkers. And whereas some argue that spirituality in education is "indoctrination" and should have no place in liberal education (Marples, 2005), others argue that spirituality is intrinsic to any classroom. Lisa Miller and Aurelie Athan (2007) claim, "From a spiritual perspective, every dimension of classroom pedagogy is part of spiritual reality; and every moment in class, a spiritual opportunity" (p. 17). Similarly, Palmer (1998/1999) states, "Spirituality—the human quest for connectedness—is not something that needs to be 'brought into' or 'added onto' the curriculum. It is at the heart of every subject we teach, where it waits to be brought forth" (p. 8).

What then are we evoking with spiritual education? Religious traditions from around the globe suggest that spirituality has to do with the inner being, with the connection between that inner self and the divine. It is not in the externals (what we eat and wear), but in the internal (who we are) that spirituality resides. Matter is fleeting, subject to decay; spirit is eternal, life-giving. We are eternal beings journeying through this transient world. Yet in contemporary thinking the dollar is king and questions of the inner life or ethics are unwelcome. The so-called "free" market controls us by excluding morality (See Cardinal Ratzinger as quoted in Anderson, 2009, p. 33). We have an inverse disconnect: *money* is what makes the world go round, and *love*, well, is never or not easily connected to how we invest our money, our time, our lives. One result is the mal/formation of children's spirituality through its commercialization in North American culture (Mercer, 2006).

The separation of body from spirit-being is troublesome. In the Christian tradition God became flesh, and therefore a body/spirit dichotomy is in fact heretical. The whole point of spirituality for a Christian and many others is that who I am in spirit will and should affect who I am in body and mind, and therefore affect how I interact with the physical and social world. And what goes on in our physical bodies affects our mood, our spirit, our way of living. Spirituality is thus embodied, lived out simultaneously in the interior and the exterior. Is everything spiritual? Indeed, yes. In the words of George MacDonald (1885), "Everything is an affair of the spirit" (p. 215). We grow in spiritual intelligence as we come to see that all of life is informed by spirituality—by the deep existential questions of the meaning of life, of self in relation to self, others, and, for many, God.

Let me describe five features of spirituality that, taken together, imply a definition of spirituality. They also imply curriculum guidelines for fostering spiritual education. I speak from a Christian perspective that grounds my outlook, but the characteristics also allow others to consider ways to include spirituality in the public classroom.

We are spiritual beings. We need to engage with the deepest questions of existence. Who am I? How and why do I matter? Do I believe God exists? If so, who is God and who am I in relation to God? How do different peoples respond to these questions?

The culture of materialism is antithetical to healthy spirituality. Making room for spirituality in the classroom is in part counter-cultural, counter to the idolatry of technology and materialism. Spirituality can affirm a deeper, richer culture.

Questions of spirituality are vital to the democratic classroom which fosters individuation of mature, independent human beings. To ignore spirituality is to elevate and even idolize materialism. To invite spirituality is to ensure scope and freedom of choice to developing moral agents. Spiritual literacy contributes to spiritual and cultural growth.

Spiritual beings are at once material beings. Who we are existentially illustrates itself in what we are materially—economically, technologically, ecologically, politically, socially.

We are works in progress. From zygote to death to eternity, we are on a journey developing into who we should become. In the imagination of Hildegard von Bingen, we arrive in this life as tightly folded tents. The process of living calls us to unfold and set it up, bit by bit, making room for growth and hope (Hildegard of Bingen, 1985).

Metaphors of Spirituality

Metaphors of spirituality in education abound. We are metaphor-making beings. We learn through analogy. Metaphorical paradigms shape us and shape culture. Iris M. Yob (1995) gleaned a number of metaphors related to spirituality from the literature: children as seekers or pilgrims; immanence—"the God within" or "the near Presence"; transcendence as that which surpasses or goes beyond immediate, empirical constructions of the world; enlightenment that brings healing; and troth or covenant. Earl MacCormac (1983) pointed to religious metaphors, such as "God acts in history," as having the power to add to, mediate, and transcend the limited metaphors of biology and culture such as "humans are animals" and "humans are machines." And Huebner (1985) identified how prevailing metaphors of growth, production, political control, and socialization hide from us our spiritual nature. In order to educate for spirituality, he advocated instead metaphors such as the lure of the transcendent, openness to the future, a consciousness which brings judgment and hope, reverence and duty, and community of care.

In thinking about teaching spirituality in public educational settings, I draw upon my discipline of literature. In particular, I will explore three interconnected metaphors: irrigating the imagination, following the invisible thread, and breaching the wall.

Irrigating the Imagination

The primary metaphor for engaging spirituality in public educational settings is one I borrow from C.S. Lewis's *The Abolition of Man* (1947): irrigating the imagination. He was concerned over how educators had succumbed to rational materialism, thereby teaching literature in an attitude of moral relativity. Instead, he urges them to educate the moral emotions so that young people will develop correct instinctive responses to good and evil. In his words, "The task of the modern educator is not to cut down jungles but to irrigate deserts. The right defence against false sentiments is to inculcate just sentiments" (p. 24). Lewis argues that children must be taught to have appropriate emotional responses to morality and immorality. We are to be humans with effectively working moral emotions, "emotions organized by trained habit into stable sentiments" (p. 34). Unless we decide to irrigate the moral imagination in the classroom, we will educate the young in a moral vacuum—and so create the conditions for the "abolition" of humanity (p. 77). This "new" human, Lewis argues, is devoid of connection with the morality rooted in all religious traditions. The inevitable result will be egotistical pleasure-seeking with the possibility of cruelty to others and even genocide. This is a drastic portrait, but C.S. Lewis is not alone in thinking that the stakes in the culture wars could not be higher.

We have all heard young (and older) people laugh cynically at violence portrayed in film or literature when they should be shocked into silence or weeping. We have all heard the stories about the hardened young who bully, even murder, without any emotional outrage or even feelings about their actions (e.g., see De Souza, 2003). In *Hold On To Your Kids* (2004), co-authors Gordon Neufeld and Gabor Maté argue that the young have exchanged the heartfelt connection that they naturally have to their parents and grandparents with peer-orientation. At an increasingly younger age and with an unprecedented velocity, Neufeld and Maté argue that the young have shifted orientation to peers so that true moral individuation is frustrated. So the rebellious young are stuck in immaturity marked by anger, rejection, denial of personal moral responsibility, and ridicule of their elders; and their elders respond with emotional retreat from the young. This "flatlining of culture" is indicative of the death of culture (p. 269).

Even if this analysis is an exaggeration, our best bet, as Neufeld and Maté suggest, is to woo our young—with saintly patience and persistence—through unconditional affirmation of their personhood (not to be confused with rewarding bad behavior), while providing moral guidance. We should attend to irrigating the emotional moral and spiritual deserts of the young. In a culture where adults seem to have lost power, this is both as exceedingly difficult as it is vital.

In irrigating the moral imagination, there are at least three features to consider: 1) choosing suitable mental furniture; 2) cultivating moral nurture of the young; 3) fostering respectful listening amongst our students.

Choosing Mental Furniture

Educators select mental furniture for their students at all times. In doing this, we need to recognize that all forms of education require "censorship": by virtue of choosing we also exclude. Both the visible and the hidden curriculums are powerful. G.K. Chesterton (1910) acknowledged this fact by asserting that all education is an act of violence (cf. Chater, 2006, p. 54); perhaps most of us are more likely to accept that education is an act of shaping. This raises the important discussion of allowing students to wrestle with ideas in order to discover for themselves what is good and what is not—and also opens the discussion on developmental psychology and the Pandora's box of what is deemed age-appropriate learning. Both confidence and discernment are in order as we choose "mental furniture."

What we *leave out* of the curriculum (often for reasons of space) is not as important as what we *put in*. We should focus on choosing works of the moral imagination that help students develop ethical responses. Teaching works we love is perhaps the best way to start. To do this, I easily turn to fairy tale because my Polish-born German mother raised me on these along with the Bible, because I dearly love fairy tales, because children can understand the nature of spirituality and morality from fictional stories, and because I believe the world of archetype is intrinsic to spiritual development. As Bruno Bettelheim, Holocaust survivor, has argued in *The Uses of Enchantment*, fairy tale is essential in helping young people discover meaning in life (1975/1977). Katherine Paterson (1987) puts it this way: "Myths and fairy tales deal directly with archetypes, and there is a very real place for them, especially as they help children to map the dark regions of their souls, to face and conquer their inner dragons. We cannot, we must not deprive children of these powerful images. Without them, not only do art and literature lose their power, but the soul itself stands ravaged and windowless like a vandalized cathedral" (p. 28). It is helpful to remember too that fairy tales were not originally considered "children's literature" in a derogatory or in any other way; they were a general cultural heritage for all people.

Fairy tales have several potential levels of meaning, as J.R.R. Tolkien (1947) has argued in "On Fairy-Stories": the natural human activity of fantasy; recovery or a re-enchantment with the world; escape from materialism; and *eucatastrophe* or consolation of the happy ending (the true form or highest function of the genre, in his view). Every fairy tale invites us to consider the moral ethos of the story. Trickster fairy tales such as *Jack and the Beanstalk* and *Mollie Whuppie* illustrate how deception and courage enable the victim to outwit and overcome the victimizer. The reward is power and status. Many others illustrate that virtue is rewarded with victory over enslavement and, often, true love. In Anderson's *Little Mermaid,* the reward for virtue leads to becoming a living soul. Many stories suggest mythical Otherness with the presence of supernatural beings and aid—the fairy godmother or the miracle-working gifts. Oscar Wilde's *The Selfish Giant* is a parable-like story of the archetypal child-leader, the Christ-child, whose meekness wins over worldly strength.

A teacher might explore questions such as the limits of self-reliance and the importance of interdependence in classic fairy tales. What is heroic? How are good and evil represented? What is the nature of passivity and activity? What is the nature of receptivity to aid? What do the gifts and the characters' responses illustrate? What is meant by "happily ever after"? How do we interpret, reinterpret, and perhaps also misinterpret fairy tales in our culture? How do these stories affirm and/or challenge key values?

The genre of fairy tale has been the site of controversy for several decades. In our money-driven world, fairy tale is often reduced to economic fantasy. The prettiest girl will be saved by the handsome and wealthy prince. Alternatively, the male and sometimes female trickster will outwit the powers of the day and thrive. Or, indeed, the particular roles are dismissed as irrelevant: these things cannot happen or they are limited to the few and cannot speak to the ordinary masses. Also, gender discourse often obscures the moral impact of fairy tale, reducing female "passivity" to less worth than male "activity." It overlooks that both genders are passive as well as active in many fairy tales, and that it is receptivity to wonder (not passivity!) that is rewarded (Hilder, 2006). These are some of the reasons why fairy tale as a teaching tool for the moral imagination is often overlooked. Beauty is conflated with materialism so that the key idea of moral beauty is missed, as Guroian describes in his comparison of original fairy tales with their Disney counterparts (1998). Instead, we might consider how the heroes represent worthy human responses—faith, hope, and love—instead of the ogre responses of self-orbiting greed. In her essay, "What is Real?", Madeleine L'Engle (1978) has discussed how fairy tale archetypes all illustrate aspects of the human psyche. We act as the "eldest" son when we are self-reliant; we act as the "youngest" son when we are willing to risk and accept help. Sometimes we speak words of gold; sometimes we have "toad days." Archetypal stories illustrate every facet of the human psyche.

How we read fairy tale, arguably, affects how we read everything else. We do and invariably will teach many of the more depressing texts that represent modern and postmodern despair and hopelessness; these are part of our cultural heritage now. But in doing so, let us also intentionally nurture the young with the vast and rich cultural heritage that speaks of ethical responsibility and hope, and sometimes suggests the supernatural. Teaching fairy tale with sensitivity to ethical and therefore spiritual formation is one form of providing healthy mental furniture.

Cultivating Moral Nurture

Second, cultivating moral nurture of the young should be central to our mission. Now some of us may have allergic reactions to the argument of "care" raised in education. True care for students that is rooted in loving-kindness, however, seeks to equip the young, to ensure that they reach for and develop their giftedness and potentially excellent passions. Writers speak of equipping young readers with imaginative literary experiences that will give them ethical, psychological, and overall spiritual strength. Genuine moral nurture is true care, and the discipline of literature is one of the best ways of achieving this (Noddings, 1984, 1992, and 2002; Hilder, 2005).

For example, in teaching Tolkien's *The Hobbit* (1937) with an eye to *The Lord of the Rings* (1954/1955), a teacher might explore how Bilbo Baggins' care about ordinary shire comforts is challenged by the task of joining forces to outwit the dragon. Why is Bilbo loathe to leave the shire? Is that immoral? What does he learn about getting along with others and his growing moral responsibility towards them? Where does his burglary fit in? Is this moral? What is heroic here? What does heroism in Bilbo tell us about true care? A continued exploration of Frodo's, Sam's, and Gollum's psychological struggles could enter the discussion. Students could be encouraged to seek out other texts (other genres, including poetry, newspaper articles, movie clips) that help us sort out the issues of care and the implications of lack of care.

None of this will help much if our students themselves are not brought to care deeply about truth. Once when I taught a ninth grade English class of 34 students (some of them unruly or indifferent), I had the magical experience of using one novel that everyone seemed to love: C.S. Lewis's *Out of the Silent Planet* (1938). It startled me to discover how much my students loved to talk about "bent" planet earth, about the spiritual beings, the eldila, on Malacandra, and about Ransom's development from fear to courage. I was surprised about their relief that at last they were "allowed" to speak and write about spirituality in a public classroom. It was safe; it was acceptable; it was their own negotiation with the text; it spoke to their deep needs and interests.

Much of our work needs to be in helping students articulate what they care about, what hurts them, how they might make healing choices in their own lives, and how much their choices matter to themselves and others.

Fostering Respectful Listening

Third, fostering respectful listening among our students is a priority for irrigating the moral imagination. Only in deep listening, based on genuine courtesy because the other has inherent value, can we find release from ego-bound perceptions and consider the large world we are part of. Discussing literature lends itself to respectful listening because any literary text offers multiple perspectives: those of the narrator, the protagonist, the antagonist, the secondary character, the unnamed stranger who doesn't appear to have a voice, and so on. All these viewpoints could be explored. Ask students, "What is that person's perspective and what motivates it? How does this other character's vision differ and contribute to knowledge?" For example, the story of the prodigal son in Luke 15 provides ground for listening to different voices. "What motivated the younger son to run away and spend his inheritance? Why did his father allow him to do so? Why did the father throw a big party on his return? What about the elder son's anger and disappointment? What does any or all of this tell us about their culture? What's subversive? How does this compare and contrast with our own cultural assumptions?" Some government literature guides allow for the inclusion of Bible passages, often in the assumed literary-rich King James version, that lend themselves to such discussions.

None of these questions may sound particularly spiritual. According to Eugene Peterson (2008), that is because Jesus used the language of indirection, similar to Emily Dickinson's vision to "Tell all the Truth but tell it slant . . . [because] The Truth must dazzle gradually / Or every man be blind . . ." (p. 5). Peterson argues that the informal conversational storytelling language of Jesus invites people inside our actual lives. Whereas the "spiritual" language of preaching or "godtalk" can objectify truth, and indeed even dress up as virtue what is really vice, the parables bring listeners to "deal personally with our family and friends in whom God is present" (p. 56). This is similar to the point made earlier, that all aspects of life are spiritual.

Like a fairy tale, a classic story like a parable also points to other texts. Katherine Paterson, for instance, speaks of her novel *The Great Gilly Hopkins* (1978) as a rewriting of the parable of the prodigal son (1989, p.12). In what other texts or media do we see the story of the parent seeking the lost child? A speaker recently linked three popular movies with this theme: *Taken* (2002), *Finding Nemo* (2003), and *The Changeling* (2008).

Respectful listening irrigates the moral imagination—through literature, for life.

Following the Invisible Thread

Related to the primary task of irrigating the moral imagination is the ethos of following the invisible thread. This metaphor is inspired by George MacDonald's novel, *The Princess and the Goblin* (1872), in which Princess Irene learns the importance of trust. Her mysterious Great-Great-Grandmother, an image of the divine, gives her a ring to which she fastens an invisible thread that is attached to the wondrous ball of thread that remains with the old woman. Irene is asked to "follow the thread wherever it leads [her]," and not to doubt the thread (p. 108). The subsequent drama of the young girl feeling her way along the thread into the heart of goblin territory inside the mountain to rescue her friend Curdie who is held hostage there, without the aid of her own rational knowledge and even contrary to her reason, is a powerful image of the importance of intuition and also faith. When she tries to follow the thread backwards—in the hope of finding a known or comfortable space—it disappears. She has no choice but to go forward into the unknown, in trust. Curdie's subsequent dismissal of the existence of her invisible thread underscores its importance. Irene succeeds precisely because she chooses trust over doubt, intuitive faith over rational control. She follows a higher reason than her own, that of the Great-Great-Grandmother, and through this discovers victory over evil. (See Hilder, 2007, for a discussion of how MacDonald's literature may help us recover spiritual discourse in education.)

It is useful to think of the quest for spirituality in the classroom as an act of following an invisible thread, of allowing students to pursue deeply meaningful questions beyond frequently perceived boundaries. Instead of asking only for known content to be mastered, we need to also make space for exploring the open-ended and the subjective. It is often observed that many students don't want to think this much; factual worksheets are easier than exploring what we make of knowledge and the nature of our existence. But perhaps if we celebrated these deeper and lasting questions, students would catch the vision for the importance of facts and the greater and more interesting value of their interpretation.

Other texts that explore intuitive knowledge abound. For example, MacDonald's fairy tale, "The History of Photogen and Nycteris" (1879), illustrates the evil of rationalism which seeks to polarize reason and imagination. Of the two forms of knowing, imagination is indeed the strength that initiates liberation. But ultimately full life is embraced in the interdependence of both. Similarly, Madeleine L'Engle's *Time* quartet underscores the dangers of self-reliant reason which imprison Charles Wallace in *A Wrinkle in Time* (1962) and similarly threaten his annihilation in *A Swiftly Tilting Planet* (1978). Instead, the characters must practice intuitive trust: Meg, for one, learns to *kythe*, to communicate with another through love beyond spoken language. In *A Wind in the Door* (1973) middle-aged Mr. Jenkins with a frozen imagination becomes a fast learner and key player. And all learn to *tesser*, to travel across time and space. Again in *Many Waters* (1986), L'Engle invites engagement with supernatural or fantastic beings, unicorns and angels, challenging rational materialism. In the words of Proginoskes in *Wind*, "Not everybody is able to see me. I'm real, and most earthlings can bear very little reality" (p. 81).

There can be no recipe for "following the invisible thread" in any one classroom. Instead it is an intuitive act initiated by the teacher that invites deepening discourse with the students. It is scary because it involves risk. But the alternative is a curriculum that shuts down exploration, and surely that is a much more frightening prospect. Willingness to undertake such risk, however, can invite spirituality into the classroom.

Breaching the Wall

A third related metaphor is that of "breaching the wall." With this image I allude to the infamous Berlin Wall which separated the people of Germany after World War II, dividing them into East and West, presumably indefinitely. But in 1989 the winds shifted and on December 31st of that year, Germans danced on top of the Berlin Wall, celebrating reunification. The unthinkable but much longed for had happened.

We have several walls that separate students from spiritual education: legal parameters and our interpretations of them, fear, indifference, and ignorance. Some facts seem too daunting, too deeply ingrained for positive change to human problems. The conclusion that "this won't change" is often read as reasonable, instead of understood as despair. But these walls need to be breached in order to educate for spirituality respectfully, ethically, academically. The human tendency is to be prescriptive, to be politically correct. We tend to "brandish the sword" rather than honor other voices. Right-wing fundamentalists (in itself a limited and limiting term) are typically accused of this, but Ben Stein's controversial documentary movie, *Expelled: No Intelligence Allowed* (2008), points to other groups who silence people. Regardless of our position, liberal education requires that we counter the assumption that "I and those who think like me are 200% right" with humility and therefore practice respectful openness to contrary views. In *King Lear,* Edgar's closing admonition, "Speak what we feel, not what we ought to say" (V. iii. 326), suggests how we can recover authentic voice and an authentic learning space for our students. Buechner (2001) uses this quotation as a starting point to search for authentic voice through deep suffering and the possibilities of faith in literature. Again, literature invites ways of "breaching the walls" that separate us from spirituality.

For example, in "The Death of Ivan Ilych" (1886), Leo Tolstoy examines the spiritual concern of living a lifetime in submission to the lure of materialism and prestige. The easy gaiety and indifference of the living, the psychological and physical agony of the dying, and the emerging possibility of faith bring the reader to the heart of spirituality. The passage when Ivan accusingly cries out to God and seems to hear an inner voice answer, "What is it you want?", raises a dramatic entry point for discussion. Similarly, Ivan's typical answer, "To live and not to suffer," invites further exploration as the God-voice responds, "To live? How?" What were Ivan's expectations? What does his life reveal? How do we as readers respond to this?

L. M. Montgomery's "Each in His Own Tongue" (1912) challenges conventional views of spirituality in formal religion. In this story the outsiders of respected society gain deep spiritual insight. All the characters along with the reader discover that God's "great, infinite forgiveness, an all-comprehending love" brings healing when a young boy allows his gift of music to speak. How does the community help or hinder spirituality? How does the individual help or hinder the community to foster spirituality?

Margaret Laurence's "The Loons" (1966) illustrates the dysfunctional relation of a largely Scots-Presbyterian community toward its ostracized Métis members. How does Dr. MacLeod challenge and transcend his community prejudice? Why does Piquette fail to receive the Christian kindness extended to her? To what extent does Christian kindness fail her? What is the nature of each character's spirituality? How does each hear or fail to hear the mocking call of the loons?

Shusako Endo's "Mothers" (1984) explores the difference between Christians who are products of "poverty, hard, grinding labor, and religious persecution" and those who have softer lives with relative security, the story of a religious mother and her prodigal son, and the view of faith through the lenses of agnosticism. How does Endo work with the tension between "Western" Christianity and Japanese experience? What is the relation of faith and rational, sophisticated theological explanation? What are the dynamics of cowardice? of duplicity? of courage?

Walter Wangerin Jr.'s "Epiphanies—Little Children Leading" (1994) speaks to the wounding that occurs in the parent-child relation. The reader is invited inside the pain and guilt of the father's mishandling of the child, of his repentance, and the son's forgiveness and consolation of the father. What does this illustrate about generational experiences and perceptions? About Wangerin's views of spirituality? Of the nature of God?

Literature seems to know few walls between human experience and spirituality. This is true of other disciplines, and the educator's task is to create space for such conversation. As the character Maddok in L'Engle's *A Swiftly Tilting Planet* (1978) comments, "People are afraid of knowledge that is not yet theirs" (p. 120). In making knowledge of spirituality available, we may breach the walls of fear.

Conclusion

So how do we enable students to irrigate their imagination, follow invisible threads, and breach the wall in the whole spectrum of curriculum subjects? For one, we do so by raising questions. How could Rwanda, where 80% of the population is Christian, suffer a tragic genocide? In what ways did 17th century Western painting deal with religious motifs? What enables us to depend on scientific laws such as the law of gravity? When it has been proven that mathematical systems cannot be both complete and consistent, what kind of faith assumptions do mathematicians have to make to develop and apply their results? How can you re-write the fairy tale, "East of the Sun and West of the Moon," from the viewpoint of the girl, the prince, one of the girl's parents, one of the girl's helpers, or one of the trolls? And how do you view her failing, her journey, and the ending? With your group of four, develop a skit about one of the following maxims: "Love isn't how you feel. It's what you do" (Proginoskes, *A Wind in the Door*, L'Engle, p. 118); "Believing takes practice" (Blajeny, *Wind*, p. 134); All that is gold does not glitter,/ Not all those who wander are lost" (Gandalf's letter, *The Fellowship of the Ring*, p. 226); or "What for you give them your beliefs?"(Jesus, "Moses Swope," Walter Wangerin Jr. p. 114). In other words, give students opportunities to use their imagination and transcend their material existence as they explore issues about the meaning of life.

Educating for spirituality is challenging, rewarding, and vital. Spirituality is not something we need to import. It's inherent to every subject. It's the essence of who we are. It needs to be given voice in the classroom. Honest and imaginative engagement with this honors our students to become mature human beings, practiced in asking the deepest questions of existence. Proselytization, in a real sense, is a moot issue. No teaching is immune from the potential of proselytization; we need to guard against this at all times. With Rilke (1903–1906) we can tell our students, "try to love *the questions themselves* . . . Don't search for the answers, which could not be given to you now, because you would not be able to live them . . . *Live* the questions now. Perhaps then, someday far into the future, you will gradually, without even noticing it, live your way into the answer" (pp. 34–35). Educating for spirituality requires patience, a love for the questions themselves, and faith in the human journey. Together with our students, let us imaginatively follow the invisible threads to weave tapestries that breach the walls of self-centeredness and materialism that are so prevalent in much of Western culture.

References

Anderson, G. (2009). Faith and finance. *First Things 193*, 29–34.

Anderson, R. (2004). *Religion and spirituality in the public school curriculum*. New York: Peter Lang.

Bettelheim, B. (1975/1977). *The uses of enchantment: The meaning and importance of fairy tales*. New York: Alfred A. Knopf.

Blake, N. (1996). Against spiritual education. *Oxford Review of Education 22*(4), 443–456.

Buechner, F. (2001). *Speak what we feel (not what we ought to say): Reflections on literature and faith*. New York: HarperCollins.

Carr, D. (1996). Songs of immanence and transcendence: A rejoinder to Blake. *Oxford Review of Education 22*(4), 457–463.

Carr, D. (1995). Towards a distinctive conception of spiritual education. *Oxford Review of Education 2*(1), 83–98.

Chater, M. (2006). Just another brick in the wall: Education as violence to the spirit. *International Journal of Children's Spirituality 11*(1), 47–56.

Chesterton, G.K. (1910/1994). Education: Or the mistake about the child. In *What's wrong with the world*, pp. 129–175. San Francisco: Ignatius Press.

Coupland, D. (1994). *Life after God*. New York: Pocket Books.

De Souza, M. (2003). Contemporary influences on the spirituality of young people: Implications for education. *International Journal of Children's Spirituality 8*(3), 269–279.

Endo, S. (1984/1987). Mothers. In J. B. Breslin, S.J. (Ed.), *The substance of things hoped for: Short fiction by modern Catholic authors* (pp. 168–96). New York: Doubleday.

Guroian, V. (1998). *Tending the heart of virtue: How classic stories awaken a child's moral imagination*. New York: Oxford University Press.

Halford, J. M. (1998/1999). Longing for the sacred in schools: A conversation with Nel Noddings. *Educational Leadership 56*(4), 28–32.

Hildegard of Bingen. (1985). *Illuminations of Hildegard of Bingen. Commentary by Matthew Fox*. Sante Fe, NM: Bear & Company.

Hilder, M. B. (2006). The 'feminine' face of heroism: Gender discourse in classic and 19th century fairy tales. Unpublished paper, ACCUTE Conference, Christianity & Literature Study Group, York University, Toronto.

Hilder, M. B. (2007). George MacDonald's education into mythic wonder: A recovery of the transcendent. In N. Duquette (Ed.), *Sublimer aspects: Interfaces between literature, aesthetics, and theology* (pp. 176–193). Newcastle, UK: Cambridge Scholars Publishing.

Hilder, M.B. (2005). Teaching literature as an ethic of care. *Teaching Education 16*(1), 43–52.

Hillis (Ed.), *The lure of the transcendent: Collected essays by Dwayne E. Huebner* (pp. 358–368). Mahwah, NJ: Lawrence Erlbaum.

Huebner, D. (1993/1999). Education and spirituality. In V. Hillis (Ed.), *The lure of the transcendent: Collected essays by Dwayne E. Huebner.* (pp. 401–416). Mahwah, NJ: Lawrence Erlbaum.

Huebner, D. (1985/1999). Religious metaphors in the language of education. In V.

L'Engle, M. (1986/2007). *Many waters.* New York: Square Fish.

L'Engle, M. (1978). *A swiftly tilting planet.* New York: Dell.

L'Engle, M .(1978). What is real? *Language Arts 55*(4), 477–51.

L'Engle, M. (1973). *A wind in the door.* New York: Dell.

L'Engle, M. (1962). *A wrinkle in time.* New York: Dell.

Laurence, M. (1966/2006). The loons. In J. C. Stott, R.E. Jones, & R. Bowers (Eds.), *The Harbrace anthology of short fiction* (4th ed., pp. 187–194). Toronto: Thomson Nelson.

Levy, S. M. (2008). *Imagination and the journey of faith.* Grand Rapids, MI: Eerdmans.

Lewis, C. S. (1947/1975). *The abolition of man or reflections on education with special reference to the teaching of English in the upper forms of schools.* New York: Macmillan.

Lewis, C. S. (1938/1974). *Out of the silent planet.* London: Pan.

MacCormac, E. (1983). Religious metaphors: Mediators between biological and cultural evolution that generate transcendent meaning. *Zygon 18*(1), 45–65.

MacDonald, G. (1885/2004). The cause of spiritual stupidity. *Unspoken sermons,* (pp. 205–221). Whitethorn, CA: Johannesen.

MacDonald, G. (1879/1999). The history of Photogen and Nycteris: A day and night Märchen. In *The complete fairy tales* (pp. 304–341). New York: Penguin.

MacDonald, G. (1872/1964). *The princess and the goblin.* Hammondsworth, England: Puffin.

Marples, R. (2005). Against faith schools: A philosophical argument for children's rights. *International Journal of Children's Spirituality 10*(2), 133–147.

Mercer, J. A. (2006). Capitalizing on children's spirituality: Parental anxiety, children as consumers, and the marketing of spirituality. *International Journal of Children's Spirituality 11*(1), 23–33.

Miller, L. and Aurelie Athan. (2007). Spiritual awareness pedagogy: The classroom as spiritual reality. *International Journal of Children's Spirituality 12*(1), 17–35.

Montgomery, L.M. (1912/1987). Each in his own tongue. In *Chronicles of Avonlea* (pp. 47–69). Toronto: Seal.

Neufeld, G. and G. Maté. (2004/2005). *Hold on to your kids: Why parents need to matter more than peers.* Toronto: Vintage.

Noddings, N. (1984). *Caring: A feminine approach to ethics and moral education.* Berkley: University of California Press.

Noddings, N. (1992). *The challenge to care in schools: An alternative approach to schools.* New York: Teachers College.

Noddings, N. (1993). *Educating for intelligent belief or unbelief.* New York: Teachers College.

Noddings, N. (2002). *Educating moral people: A caring alternative to character education.* New York: Teachers College.

Palmer, P. (1983). *To know as we are known: A spirituality of education.* New York: Harper & Row.

Palmer, P. J. (1998/1999). Evoking the spirit in public education. *Educational Leadership 56*(4), 6–11.

Paterson, K. (1987). *The great Gilly Hopkins.* New York: HarperTrophy.

Paterson, K. (1989). *The spying heart: More thoughts on reading and writing books for children*. New York: E.P. Dutton.

Peterson, E. H. (2008). *Tell it slant: A conversation on the language of Jesus in his stories and prayers*. Grand Rapids, MI: Eerdmans.

Pinar, W. F., W. M. Reynolds, P. Slattery, P.M. Taubman (1995/2000). *Understanding curriculum: An introduction to the study of historical and contemporary curriculum discourses*. New York: Peter Lang.

Radford, M. (2003). Emotional intelligence and education. *International Journal of Children's Spirituality 8*(3), 255–268.

Rilke, R. M. (1903–1908/1986). *Letters to a young poet* (Stephen Mitchell, Trans.). New York: Random House.

Smith, D. (2000). Secularism, religion and spiritual development. *Journal of Beliefs & Values: Studies in Religion & Education 21*(1), 27–38.

Tolkien, J. R. R. (1954/55/1977). *The fellowship of the ring*. Agincourt, ON: Methuen.

Tolkien, J. R. R. (1937/1975). *The hobbit*. London: Unwin.

Tolkien, J. R. R. (1947/1977). On fairy-stories. *The Tolkien reader* (pp. 3–73). New York: Ballantine.

Tolstoy, L. (1886/2007). The death of Ivan Ilych (Louside and Aylmer Maude, Trans.). In X. J. Kennedy and D. Gioia (Eds.), *An introduction to fiction* (10th ed., pp. 280–317). New York: Longman.

Van Brummelen, H., Koole, R., & Franklin, K. (2004). Transcending the commonplace: Spirituality in the curriculum. *Journal of Educational Thought 38*(3), 237–253.

Wangerin Jr., Walter. (1994). Epiphanies—little children leading. In *Ragman: And other cries of faith* (pp. 15–22). New York: HarperCollins.

Wangerin Jr., Walter. (1994). Moses Swope. In *Ragman: And other cries of faith* (pp. 106–16). New York: HarperCollins.

Whitehead, A. N. (1929/1949). *The aims of education: And other essays*. New York: New American library.

Yob, I. M. (1995). Spiritual education: A public school dialogue with religious interpretations. *Religious Education 90*(1), 104–117.

nine

Metaphors and Models
of Faith-Learning Integration

Ken Badley

WALKING INTO A CLASSROOM in a Christian secondary school, I see a large poster on the wall with these words from Philippians 4:8: "Whatever is true, whatever is honorable, whatever is just, whatever is pure, whatever is pleasing, whatever is commendable . . . think about these things." The poster prompts me to wonder about several questions. First, I wonder how effective large classroom posters are, whether they portray the solar system, chart the history of the European Union, or repeat an important biblical teaching. Do students in Christian schools become inoculated against Paul's words in the same way that science students no longer notice the Periodic Table of the Elements in their classroom? But this poster in a Christian school classroom also leads me to wonder about the ways in which the faith commitment of Christian teachers affects the teaching and learning in both Christian and public school classrooms. What ways do they find to express their faith and to communicate to students that they consider some choices better than others, some loyalties more worthy than others, some interpretations more valid than others? What metaphors come to their mind for the connections they wish to make between faith and learning?

Teachers in both public and Christian schools want to know how to realize—to live out—their faith commitments in their classrooms. Given the legal constraints within which they work, Christian teachers in public schools especially wonder what is the wisest yet effective path to follow. What may they do? What may they say? Teachers in Christian schools face some of the same and some different challenges as public school teachers. Some educators in Christian schools hang Bible verse posters on their classroom walls. Others go much deeper. They seek to ground every aspect of their school vision, curriculum, and pedagogy deeply in a Christian world and life view. Some no doubt see the first as a valid expression of the second, but others consider Bible texts or Christian slogans to be superficial sloganeering. Christians working in public education have their own strategies. Some talk about being salt to preserve and give flavor to the world, following the Sermon on the Mount (recorded in Matthew 5:13). Some view themselves as quiet witnesses to God's love, perhaps following a comment St. Francis of Assisi is reported to have made that we should preach the gospel at all times, using words if necessary. These are but two of the many ways that teachers in public schools have understood God's call on their lives as professional teachers.

For several decades, many educators and scholars have used the phrase *faith-learning integration* to refer to these questions and the challenge of finding biblical ways to connect Christian faith with what happens in classrooms. Protestant evangelicals and fundamentalists have found the phrase especially attractive since Frank Gaebelein, a school principal in New York State, used it in his book, *The Pattern of God's Truth* (Gaebelein, 1954). Reformed educators have also used the phrase, as have some Roman Catholic and a few mainline Christian educators. Of course, the question and the challenge it represents are much older than the particular phrase, but the phrase has become popular enough to justify our exploring it here.

Conduct a quick search on the web and you will discover that some who use this phrase believe there to be only one approach to faith-learning integration: theirs. I have followed this conversation for several decades and have observed that different Christian educators have taken a variety of approaches to the question of living faith-fully in schools and classrooms. Not all those approaches go by the same name, although many people use the language of faith-learning integration.

Richard Niebuhr, a theologian, suggested sixty years ago that throughout history Christians had found Scriptural warrant for five different answers to the question of how Christ and culture relate to each other. In *Christ and Culture* (1951), Niebuhr differentiates these models: Christ against culture, the Christ of culture, Christ the transformer of culture, Christ and culture in paradox, and Christ above culture. Niebuhr labeled these models quite accurately and I will not describe them in more detail here (but do recommend two related and recent volumes: Carter, 2007; Crouch, 2008). I mention Niebuhr and his famous book here to remind us all that people who wished to follow God have always asked how to live wisely and faithfully in this world. All Christians, in both public and church-related settings, face this old question. Some reflect on the question using the language of faith-learning integration and many do not.

Whether they teach in public schools or Christian schools, Christian educators can navigate this territory with God's guidance, the right map, a sense of intellectual adventure, and sufficient spiritual humility to believe that others might have legitimate insights into the ways that God works in our world. My specific goal in this chapter is to unfold some of the maps—metaphors really—that Christian educators use as they navigate this territory.

Curriculum Metaphors and Models of Faith-Learning Integration

In 1986, when I completed my doctoral dissertation on how educators use the phrase faith-learning integration, I argued that the faith-learning debate largely took place between five models; at that time, I called these incorporation, fusion, correlation, dialogical, and perspectival. When I submitted my dissertation, I believed that these five models were the five models of faith and learning integration; that is, there were no more ways to connect faith and learning. Now, I see that they form a cluster of metaphors that focus mostly on knowledge and the contents of the curriculum. I now call them curricular and epistemological models of faith-learning integration and see them as one family of models among others. If I could rewrite my dissertation today, I would point to several other quite different models and I would offer more pointed criticisms of the five I distinguished. I will describe some of these other models later in this chapter. First, I will summarize and review each of the curricular and epistemological models I originally distinguished in my thesis.

Very simply, in incorporation integration educators are to meld one subject or content area into another. Examples today include the concern that teachers attend to environmental awareness, technological proficiency or literacy and numeracy in all subject areas of the curriculum.

In the parallel case of faith and learning, incorporation might mean that the classroom teacher seeks ways to introduce considerations of faith questions in a mathematics or social studies class. On the surface, this metaphor seems to exclude teachers in public school settings but I will raise the question of explicit and implicit incorporation later in the chapter in a way that will keep this door open to Christian teachers in the public school classroom. Many find this metaphor or model of faith and learning easy to grasp because it works in exact parallel to other forms of curriculum incorporation such as the examples I provided.

Incorporation may, in fact, be easier to grasp than to realize in appropriate ways. First there is the temptation to superficiality. I think of a Christian school that required every lesson plan to include a Bible verse (not necessarily related to the lesson) at the top of the page. I asked a teacher from that school if she thought of printing sheets of Bible verse stickers and simply peeling one label off for each lesson to make the point that the exercise had such potential for superficiality. She answered that the school's leaders would be pleased that she had done advanced planning. My response was that Genesis 27:11, which reads "My brother Esau is a hairy man, but I am a smooth man," must certainly belong somewhere in such a school. A second error awaits those who might think incorporation a simple process: obtrusiveness. Having taught in a Christian secondary school for nine years, I know that students become jaded about teachers who, as students view it, push Jesus down their throats. Theologically, we know that God's grace and God's claims do reach to every corner of the curriculum and every minute of the school day. But that theological principle should not dictate a pedagogy that drives students away from loving God.

Fusion designates a second model of curriculum integration that parallels how some understand faith-learning integration. In fusion integration, two subjects of the curriculum are combined into one course, for example in general science courses which combine subject matter from biology, chemistry, and physics. Following the parallel, some Christians talk about infusing biblical faith into every corner and aspect of the curriculum and the school program. Their objective in calling for such infusion is clear, but I have concluded that the fusion metaphor does not suit faith and learning integration very well because faith is so much more than or different from subject-area contents or a body of disciplinary knowledge; faith is not just a set of propositions. The two elements in the *faith and learning* phrase are not as alike as are biology, chemistry, and physics. If anything, those calling for the degree of infusion I have described here may simply be calling for a saturation degree of incorporation, the curricular model I briefly described just above.

Those who call for *correlation* integration in curriculum discussions envision students, teachers or textbook authors pointing out connections between subject contents. In this model of integration, the student reading a novel might notice that she studied some of the details of that novel's historical setting in her social studies class. Such interdisciplinary links enhance learning, of course, and some teachers teach intentionally so that students can discover and make the links. Some of the problems encountered by those advocating fusion models of faith-learning integration seem to be solved by this correlation model. To the degree that the Christian worldview is a comprehensive vision of the world, God's purposes for it, and our life in it, we should be able to identify connections between aspects of Christian faith and every content area of the curriculum.

A friend who teaches chemistry uses the ephedra plant in a way that illustrates this model of faith-learning integration. Speaking theologically, the ephedra plant is like all plants, a gift of God and part of God's creation. The Chinese have used ephedra as a decongestant for thousands of years, and pharmaceutical manufacturers today use it to produce commercial decongestants. Like all of God's gifts, the ephedra plant can be used for good or ill. Yet, as many know, ephedrine is used to manufacture crystal meth, one of the most addictive and destructive drugs ever produced. Thus, ephedra has the power to heal or to destroy, and it thereby offers the wise teacher a powerful curricular venue for discovering a connection point between biology or chemistry, and such larger questions as God's gifts to this world and God's purposes for this world. Not all curricular contents offer such obvious or powerful points of correlation, but teachers and students willing to search and willing to live in wonder can discover great curricular and theological rewards. When they make such connections as these, they discover or demonstrate the power of correlation models of faith and learning.

The very strength that correlation models have with reference to curriculum contents may mean that they come up short in other areas. Because curriculum contents seem to offer themselves as the easiest candidates for making correlations, correlation models may cause educators to overlook the reality that Christian faith also has everything to do with attitudes and values, with the purposes of schools, and with the thousands of simple interactions between teachers and students that happen in a typical week. While this model bears good fruit, it does so only in a limited area. In fact, it was the limits of correlation metaphors that caused me some years ago to begin to understand the limited usefulness of having only five models of faith-learning integration, all of them focused on epistemology and the curriculum.

When I conducted the research for my doctoral dissertation, I discovered that a number of people talking about faith and learning seemed to envision a dialogue. This *dialogical* model is more closely related to correlation than to the incorporation and fusion models I outlined above. The dialogue in question is between those who follow Christian faith (and followers of other religious faiths as well) and practitioners or theorists in any school subject, academic discipline or field of research. The dialogue often focuses on ethical questions so that, for example, some Christians ask if physicians should use a given procedure just because it has the potential to heal (think of the stem-cell debate, for example). Others who tend toward dialogical metaphors of faith and learning might focus on questions of the ultimate purposes of human life, the proper role of the state or family, or the origins of the earth. These questions—on which reasonable people do not all agree—provide sites for dialogue and mutual listening. Teachers in some Christian schools and some public schools have the luxury of engaging students in such dialogue. Other teachers, in both Christian and public schools, have no such luxury, and in fact may be prohibited from entering any such dialogue, creating for such teachers significant pedagogical challenges.

I noted that the metaphor of dialogue overlaps with the metaphor of correlation. Both those models overlap with the last of the models I identified in my doctoral work: *perspectival* integration. In this model, the world of study makes sense because the student or teacher views it from a specific perspective or from the vantage point of a particular worldview. Some books about Christian worldviews, for example, make the claim that, viewed from a Christian perspective, the whole world makes sense. Some authors apply that claim specifically to the world of study. St. Paul wrote about taking "every thought captive to obey Christ" (II Corinthians 10:5), a phrase that has now appeared in the title of several books about Christian perspectives on study and the academy (Gill, 1989; Hermann, 1985; King, 2011). Paul also wrote that in Christ "all things hold together"

(Colossians 1:17), apparently a quotation from a gospel song popular in first century churches. biblical scholars believe that Paul was making reference there to the physical universe, but the connection to models of faith-learning integration is unavoidable. From a Christian perspective, the whole curriculum holds together and finds coherence. But on this perspectival account it makes sense only when we view it through the lens of Christian faith. This coherence should not lead to pride or self-satisfaction, however; we should remember St. Paul's warning that we see imperfectly (I Corinthians 13:12) and our understanding of any subject in the curriculum will remain imperfect until we see face to face. Thus, both curricular humility and interdisciplinary conversation are in order, as well as discussions about how scholars who are not Christian have also given us deep insights into the multidimensional issues of life and culture.

Here then are five models or metaphors of faith and learning integration: incorporation, fusion, correlation, dialogue, perspective. Each of these envisions a different though not mutually exclusive kind of relationship between faith and learning. Some might want to know which of these models is right, or at least which model is best? I will avoid answering that question at this point because I think they all miss an important aspect of Christian faith—that Christian faith, while it does have a cognitive aspect, is not only about assent to a body of teachings or doctrines. It is not only about making sense of a curriculum from this or that perspective. Christian faith—or should I say *the Christian life?*—also involves practices, the will and the emotions (concerns addressed in a book that appeared just before this book went to press, Smith, Smith, Bass, & Dykstra, 2011). Christian faith means living out the Christian Story, something more encompassing and much richer than living by doctrines of faith. I noted in the introduction to these five models that I view them as curricular or epistemological models because they tend to focus on knowledge and its organization. Obviously, models of faith-learning integration do need to take epistemological questions into account, but they need to do much more than that.

Personal and Spiritual Metaphors
of Faith-Learning Integration

Many participants in the faith-learning discussion focus on Christian character and personal transformation within teachers and students. I call these *personal/spiritual* models. I think of a kindergarten teacher in a public school who prays on her way to school each day for each of the children in her class. By no means is this all she does to carry out her God-given vocation to teach, but she has done it faithfully for several decades. Such prayers, in my view, are one part of her effort to realize—to make real—what many people call faith and learning integration. Whether she uses that language or not, she wants her kindergarten pupils to feel safe and valued in her classroom, and she wants them to experience joy and wonder in learning. Because she teaches in a public school, she perhaps will never tell her pupils about Christ. But she attempts to show them Christ every day and she prays in part that God would allow her to do exactly that. I am sure that many other Christian teachers pray in the same way. In the summary of incorporation models of integration, I noted the continuum running from implicit to explicit. Inasmuch as the teacher I am describing here does not say in so many words that the values she wants to shape her teaching and classroom are Christian values, she has adopted a more implicit model of faith-learning integration, On the other hand, if you walked into her classroom, you would sense in two minutes that something deep, rich, and Christian shapes all that happens there. In that sense, this teacher's faith is quite explicit; it is on display every moment of every day, although the display may remain unlabelled, so to speak, week after week and year after year.

Many of the teachers who want to make their faith real in their class-room believe that their actions far outweigh any lessons they might plan or words they might say. For them, personal character—which is always on display—is where faith and learning connect (and, in some cases, fail to connect). For some of these teachers, teacher character may trump coherent curriculum. I have heard a few teachers claim that curriculum does not matter at all, that character is everything, but they are a small minority. Most teachers who claim that teacher character is the most obvious proving ground for faith also believe that faith impinges significantly on curriculum and pedagogical strategies. My informal observation over decades bears out what Matthias found in her formal research on Christian professors' models of faith and learning integration (Matthias, 2007). She discovered that many teachers combine behind-the-scenes practices such as prayer with classroom practices and content that speak of peace, hope, and respect. We recognize these as ideals at which many teachers aim regardless of their religious framework but which many Christian teachers see as integral parts of expressing and realizing winsome Christian faith within their teaching and classrooms. As it happens, Matthias conducted her research at Wheaton College, an openly Christian setting. My personal experience suggests that her findings apply as well to many thousands of Christians working in public education.

Already in this chapter, I have pointed out that different educators view and enact the relationship of faith and learning in varied ways. This further dimension on which Christian educators differ relates to how openly teachers should be or are in their classrooms about their faith commitments. How *explicit* or *implicit*—how openly or discretely do Christian educators live their Christian lives, especially in public settings? An implicit-explicit continuum might run from outright denial on one end (like that of St. Peter, recorded in Luke 22:57) through just out of sight, to active proselytizing or even indoctrination (or even terror and unvarnished compulsion) on the other end. As I noted above with reference to the kindergarten teacher who prays for her students, the terms *explicit* and *implicit* themselves may not catch all the nuances in the question we should be asking here. Clearly, some might view the continuum only with reference to whether and how much an individual talks about his or her faith. Others might say that the teacher in my example shows her faith and therefore makes it more than implicit. I will not try to serve as referee in that linguistic contest but I do want my readers to notice the range of approaches Christians might take, and some of the difficulties we encounter even when we try to name those approaches. I will also not use this chapter to recommend specific paths for the Christian teacher in the Christian school or public school classroom, a task that others have done quite ably already (Stronks & Stronks, 1999; Van Brummelen, 2009). Rather, I would like to explore what different teachers' metaphors and models reveal about how they think about the available paths and this territory.

A Christian teaching in a public school once told me that he viewed himself as a *secret service agent*. In contrast, I have heard a number of people say that the Christian who teaches in a public setting is actually a *missionary*. When we unpack such terms as these we might be left with more questions than answers. Regarding the first image, we might ask if anyone at all knows the secret agent's deepest loyalties? Are today's laws in various jurisdictions so stringent that they forbid the teacher ever from revealing his or her convictions about the deepest questions humans ask? (Monica Hilder also deals with these questions in her chapter in this volume.) Is a commitment to Christ so different from concern for the biosphere or loyalty to Toyota that one is forbidden from mentioning the one but free to mention the other two?

The term *missionary* raises quite different questions. Do missionaries only talk to people they wish to reach with their message or do they also listen to the people among whom they find themselves? Can Christians who teach in public settings bear witness to Christ's love for the world in ways other than talking, ways such as showing love, care, and respect? Backing up one more step, do Christian teachers not show Christ's love by simply teaching: by helping students learn to read, count, understand waves, appreciate the complexities of history or love the world they live in? Are these not gifts the teacher can give in the name of Christ, even if circumstances prevent her saying that name aloud? Does the Christian who openly proselytizes in a public classroom where such activity is forbidden honor God by ignoring the laws in place in that jurisdiction? I don't pretend that these questions are simple, especially in light of the writers of Scripture having made so clear that God's people are to spread the Good News. Readers may find one or the other (or both) of the images of secret service agent and missionary offensive. I include them simply to illustrate the variety of metaphors that Christians in public settings use to describe and help understand their work, especially the complex question of how to live and teach faithfully in public settings.

One recent researcher made the question of openness about Christian faith the focus of her doctoral research with nine pre-service teachers who completed five months of pre-service teaching in public schools (Franklin, 2010). She asked her participants to tell how they navigated the tension between concealing and revealing their Christian faith. In her view, that question brings into view issues of ethics and teacher integrity as well as conformity and teacher identity. Because of the semantic richness of the metaphor of *veiling*, Franklin asked her nine participants to tell their stories with reference to veiling and she used veiling to interpret their stories. Perhaps all Christians who teach in public settings should find a workable metaphor for their approaches to the question of concealing and revealing. For some, Franklin's veil may offer needed insights. Others will doubtless find other metaphors.

Images such as *secret service agent* and *missionary* (and perhaps even *veil*), which help us see the range of perspectives on openness about faith in public places, may prevent our noticing an important social-psychological reality. Whether we think about faith commitments, favorite novels or preferences in cars, we know that some people hold and live out their views in winsome and inviting ways and other people hold and live out their views in offensive and repulsive ways. Thomas Groome, well known Christian educator, notes that "even the best teaching methods will be less effective and perhaps defeated if an educator's presence in learners' lives is a negative one, for example, if the educator is authoritarian, elitist, manipulative, mean, or biased" (2011, p. 29). Sadly, we have all met the teachers that Groome describes. I tried to show that the explicit/implicit continuum can help us understand the questions at hand, even with its potential for ambiguity and causing confusion. In light of Groome's comment, we should perhaps also develop a second continuum that runs from winsome to offensive for it would catch another important dimension of faithful living in the world of schools and classrooms, both Christian and public.

Providentially, thousands of positive, winsome Christian teachers represent Christ in schools everywhere. They bring to class their care, their sense of humor, their respect for ideas, students and colleagues, their loving manner of living and speaking, their wonder and curiosity. We have all met such people. They often leave us wondering how they manage to maintain their positive vision of life; perhaps we even wonder how we could become more like them. Think of the people Groome listed on one end of a continuum and these winsome, welcoming Christians on the other end. Believers from across this range (or nearly across it) represent Christ—for good or ill—every day in classrooms and in all the other places that people work, gather and learn. In the decades of conversation about faith-learning integration, few have taken serious note of this winsome /offensive continuum. The common faith-learning metaphors deflect our attention away from this important dimension of Christian living and educating. In doing so, these metaphors may confirm Lakoff and Johnson's thesis, but, more importantly, they may lead us to miss the most important things we must do—and be—as Christian teachers.

I suspect that the metaphors of secret agent and missionary rarely come to mind for these thousands of teachers who bring grace and humor to their classrooms and show their students care and respect. More likely, they see themselves as the salt of the earth, people who help preserve their society from decay. Many use the language of service; they teach so that they might serve the wider human community. They believe that when they serve students by helping them make needed progress in their learning, they also serve Christ, who said at one point that doing good things for the "least of these" was, in effect, doing those things for him (Matthew 25:40). People in the inner-city church I attend often use this passage to refer to the homeless people we serve. I believe that many school children also fit this category, and when Christian teachers direct their life's energy and their teaching gifts toward school children, Christ views their work as if it were done unto him.

To conclude this discussion of personal and spiritual models of faith-learning integration, we should remember the many Christian educators who use the language of vocation (from the Latin word for *voice*). These teachers have heard a voice that called them into teaching. For them, teaching is a response to a call. Without disparaging the connections that Christian faith might have to curriculum contents, they go to work each day aware that faith has everything to do with how they plan, teach, and assess students. And they also go to work each day aware that how they are Christian—their Christian character—has everything to do with their effectiveness as teachers, to recall Groome's comment. My readers might be able to generate a better label than I have done for such models of faith and learning, but I call these personal and spiritual models of faith-learning integration.

Pedagogical Metaphors and Models of Faith-Learning Integration

The curriculum metaphors and personal/spiritual models I have discussed so far do not exhaust all the ways people envision connecting faith and education. Some educators have suggested that faith-learning integration happens best in classrooms where the teacher has created a certain climate or *ethos* which honors Christ or points to Christ's presence. Related to classroom climate, some say that faith and learning connect when teachers recognize and use those *teaching moments* that simply arise in the course of every day. I call these families of metaphors of faith-learning integration *pedagogical models*.

I will explore the ethos models first. Year after year, I ask pre-service teachers to describe their desired classroom ethos or climate. I ask them to list a maximum of ten properties or qualities. Over several years, my students have helped me develop a rather lengthy list of terms, a portion of which I will repeat here: accountability, authenticity, beauty, care, celebration, collaboration, communication, compassion, confidence, co-operation, courage, creativity, curiosity, dedication, differentiation, empathy, engagement, environmental awareness, excitement, fairness, forgiveness, freedom, fun, grace, gratitude, group-work, honesty, hope, hospitality, imagination, integrity, joy, justice, kindness, laughter, learning, love, open-mindedness, patience, peace, perseverance, purpose, respect, responsibility, reverence for ideas, rewards, risk-taking, routines, safety, self-assessment, self-control, self-direction, service, *shalom*, support, team-work, transparency, trust, truth-telling, volunteerism, welcoming, and wonder. What teachers would not want these properties and qualities to characterize their classroom!

Readers may have noticed that some of these precise terms appear in Scripture, in passages such as Galatians 5:22–23, where Paul lists what he calls the fruit of the Spirit: love, joy, peace, patience, kindness, generosity, faithfulness, gentleness, and self-control (NRSV). Other ideals, while not from Scripture, still illustrate that teachers who want to connect faith and learning will identify specific ways in which to make those connections. For them, faith and learning connect not in some general or abstract sense, but in the very atmosphere they work to create in their classrooms. As they give their energy day to day in the core cycle of teaching work—curriculum, planning, instruction, and assessment—all teachers create with their students one kind of ethos or another. For each of the ideals I have listed in the paragraph above, teachers who want to integrate faith and learning engage in specific practices to realize those ideals. That is, if because I am Christian I want my classroom to be characterized by justice and kindness (to pick just two), then I will need to aim to realize those ideals in the specific aspects of the work I do as a teacher. The main aspects of my work as a teacher involve curriculum, instruction, and assessment (and of course such matters as taking attendance, lunch-room duty, attending student activities, and so on). To live into this model of faith-filled teaching or faith-learning integration I will need to be intentional about realizing justice and kindness in all the moments of my teaching day, especially as I engage in the activities of the core cycle. In chapter 2 on "Metaphors for Learners," Carla Nelson and I explore this further, when we ask how teachers strive to achieve consistency—what many educators now call alignment—between their ideals and their teaching practice.

Pre-service teachers generated the list of qualities I provided above. Their lists of classroom ideals typically overlap with the lists of desired qualities offered by educational leaders and policy makers. For example, in the book where he described his vision for K–12 education, Ernest Boyer (1995) listed respect, giving, honesty, responsibility, compassion, self-discipline, and perseverance. Boyer believed that schools could help students live into these virtues through curriculum, through classroom climate and through service. William Bennett, who once served as Secretary of Education in the United States, offered a list that included the last five qualities listed by Boyer, as well as loyalty, faith, work, friendship, and courage (Bennett, 1993).

We probably expect these educators' lists to overlap with those assembled by the teacher candidates I work with or with similar lists that you might produce if you took the time to do so (I recommend you limit yourself initially to naming ten qualities). My point in reviewing such lists of virtues and desired classroom qualities is that good teachers know that educators cannot simply pull classroom climate out of the air. They recognize that classroom climate—healthy or not—is built in and through a thousand teaching moments and interactions. Climate begins with the teacher's own demonstration of the qualities and virtues she desires. It entails helping students recognize, understand and live out of the desired qualities, even when easier paths may present themselves. To return to the language of models and metaphors of faith-learning integration, many teachers who adopt pedagogical models of faith and learning integration focus on the virtues and qualities I have listed here as ways to manifest that integration. And they know that the time to live out those qualities and virtues is in every teaching moment of every day.

In a recent conversation about ideals and classrooms, a teacher told me that she considers it her job to create a *generative space*, by which she meant a space where students and their teachers can succeed at generating their best, most creative work. Not having heard that phrase before,

I searched it online and discovered that the phrase did not originate in education but in medicine. I like it, and see connections to Parker Palmer's use of spatial language in *To Know as We are Known* (1983). As new phrases usually do, it forced me to think new thoughts. I believe that most good teachers could warm to the concept of a classroom as a generative space. As it happens, the teacher who first used that phrase in my presence spoke from a foundation of Christian faith and I believe may have caught part of the educational ideal of those who have grown tired of the phrase, *the integration of faith and learning*. This new phrase allows or maybe forces us to ask what we want to generate or what we want our students to generate. And by asking what it is we want to generate, it encourages us as teachers to think about the end results of our work, not just about the next tasks that we need to finish.

The image of a generative space invites a couple more questions as well, which, as a Christian, I like. First, it invites me to ask what I want God to generate in me and in my students. Have I planned the kind of work for us that will allow us to notice God's role in this world and God's invitation for us to participate in the Divine plan? I am not suggesting here that my classroom become a place where I evangelize my students. But I am asking whether the kind of atmosphere I create with my students will create openings for my students and God to find each other. Second, the phrase connects with the theological concept of *regeneration*, which relates to the work that God does within those who name Christ. Scriptural writers did not use this term and we do not hear it much today. But as a teacher of children or adults who are precious in God's sight, I welcome the reminder that my classroom might serve as a place where Divine encounters lead to new growth in people's lives. If the metaphor of a generative space can remind me of such matters, it is a metaphor I should keep at the forefront of my thinking about teaching.

Pedagogical models and metaphors of faith and learning focus on the thousands of weeks, days, moments, and micro-moments in classrooms during which teachers respond in one way or another to student comments and behaviors, to interruptions, to brilliant answers and wrong answers, and to all the joys and sorrows that fill our days and our students' days. Pedagogical models are not necessarily opposed to the epistemological and curricular models I surveyed at the start of the chapter. They obviously overlap in significant ways with the spiritual and personal models I surveyed in the second part of the chapter. And they remind us that every moment that we work as teachers we construct an ethos that speaks of Christ's presence and goodness or we construct something else.

Institutional Metaphors and Models

Finally, some have described what I call institutional models of faith-learning integration. What is the school's mission? In what conceptual framework does it carry out its work? Just as every teacher builds and shapes a classroom climate, every school also builds a climate or ethos, whether it means to or not.

The power—and the beauty—of school climate struck me with great force during a visit I made to an elementary school in Peterborough, Ontario. After meeting me briefly in his office before the school day, the principal said to me, "Time to head outside." I followed him outdoors and then watched, amazed, as he greeted every car and bus that pulled up in the school's front driveway. Morning recess saw us out there again, with the principal engaged in conversation with children from every grade. As I watched him throughout the day, I couldn't help but recall the sociological concept of *social capital*, thinking that he would have a deep pool of goodwill if and when he needed to speak firmly about an issue, enforce a policy, or lead the school through a difficult change. But as I followed and watched him interact with students, staff and parents I realized that he didn't engage people in this way to build social capital. He did it to build an ethos, in this case a deeply Christian ethos characterized by joy, wonder, hospitality, and care. From our conversation, I know he also had a thoroughly Christian understanding of curriculum. But if I were forced to check just one box on a survey called "Preferred model of faith-learning integration," I would need to say that in Rhema Christian School, faith had saturated and shaped every aspect of the school's operations.

How is this principal's approach to making Christian faith real different from the models of faith-learning integration I have described so far in this chapter? I'm sure that it overlaps with many of the approaches I have discussed. Perhaps it simply illustrates at an institutional level some of the personal/spiritual and pedagogical models I have described for individuals. The key difference of course is that here we are talking about building an ethos in a whole school, not just in one classroom. If we were able to ask students and alumni (or even parents and teachers) connected to Rhema Christian School to describe the atmosphere there or the essence of what makes the school great, some might answer simply, "It is Christian." To those who answered that way, we could ask a follow-up question, "What do you mean by 'Christian'?" They might then say that the school is characterized by kindness, respect and caring, or dozens of other qualities. Some might say that the school has a chapel service, or that some classes start with prayer, or that some classrooms have Bible verses posted on the wall, but most would see that Rhema's Christian character runs far beyond those easily visible features. I suspect that many—students, parents and teachers alike—would say something about the principal. His actions, which embody specific educational ideals and attitudes, inspire the whole institution.

This single vignette, from a single school, illustrates what I have concluded about institutional models and metaphors of integration. Institutions are comprised of people, and the people make and shape the institution. Any models or metaphors for faith and learning integration we might name for institutions will likely differ only in scale from what we hope all Christian educators attempt to realize in their individual classrooms. Interestingly, Frank Gaebelein, the author who popularized faith-learning integration language back in 1954, reserved the word integration for the kind of institution-wide faith-filled-ness I am discussing here (Gaebelein, 1954). Not to close the circle too tightly, but Harro Van Brummelen, my co-editor of this volume and the author of the chapter on metaphors for assessment that also appears here, envisions the same kind of comprehensive faith-shaped schools in *Walking with God in the Classroom* (2009).

Conclusion

Throughout this book, we have seen the wide range of metaphors educators use for various aspects of education. We know that different educators find different metaphors attractive for various reasons, one of which is usually that different educators have differing visions of the meaning of life and the purposes of schools. Certainly in the case of faith-learning metaphors, different educators' understandings of how Christ relates to culture will lead them to favor one metaphor over another. Personality factors also play a role, but this chapter is not the right place to launch an archeological expedition into the psychological dimensions of teachers' choices of metaphors.

In this chapter, I have focused mainly on three kinds of models or metaphors for bringing Christian faith to bear on educational tasks: epistemological and curricular models, personal and spiritual models, and pedagogical models. In my ideal vision of education, teachers come to school with both their classes and their souls prepared. In other words, I consider the personal and spiritual models necessary and foundational, whether one teaches in a church-related school or a public school. But I do not consider that foundation sufficient. The edifice of day-to-day educational work that the teacher builds on top of that foundation must also be deeply Christian. With that foundation, the teacher brings faith to all the moments of the teaching year, in all the aspects of curriculum, planning, instruction, assessment, and nurturing a caring and supportive learning community. In short, the personal and spiritual models underlie and underwrite curricular and epistemological models as well as pedagogical models of faith and learning integration. The teacher who can work back and forth among these three models can approach all that goes on through the school day in a thoroughly Christian way, whether that school names Christ or not.

References

Bennett, W. J. (Ed.). (1993). *The book of virtues: A treasury of great moral stories*. New York: Simon & Schuster.

Boyer, E. L. (1995). *The basic school: A community for learning*. Princeton, NJ: Carnegie Foundation for the Advancement of Teaching.

Carter, C. (2007). *Rethinking Christ and culture*. Grand Rapids, MI: Baker.

Crouch, A. (2008). *Culture making: Recovering our creative calling*. Downers Grove, IL: InterVarsity.

Franklin, K. (2010). *The dialogical relationship between spiritual and professional identity in beginning teachers: Context, choices and consequences*. Unpublished doctoral dissertation, Simon Fraser University, Burnaby, BC.

Gaebelein, F. (1954). *The pattern of God's truth: The integration of faith and learning*. New York: Oxford.

Gill, D. W. (1989). *The opening of the christian mind: Taking every thought captive to christ*. Downers Grove: Inter-Varsity.

Groome, T. (2011). *Will there be faith?: A new vision for educating and growing*. New York: HarperOne.

Hermann, K. W. (1985). *Every thought captive to Christ: A guide to resources for developing a Christian perspective in the major academic disciplines*. Kent, OH Radix Christian Studies Program.

King, D. W. (2011). *Taking every thought captive: Forty years of Christian Scholar's Review*. Abilene, TX: Abilene Christian University Press.

Matthias, L. R. (2007). *Dual citizenship in Athens and Jerusalem: A portrait of professors who exemplify the integration of faith and learning at Wheaton College (Illinois)*. Unpublished doctoral dissertation, Regent University, Virginia Beach, VA.

Niebuhr, H. R. (1951). *Christ and culture*. New York: Harper.

Palmer, P. (1983). *To know as we are known: A spirituality of education*. San Francisco: Harper.

Smith, D. I., Smith, J. K. A., Bass, D., & Dykstra, C. (2011). *Teaching and Christian practices: Reshaping faith and learning*. Grand Rapids, MI: Eerdmans.

Stronks, G. G., & Stronks, J. K. (1999). *Christian teachers in public schools: A guide for teachers, administrators, and parents*. Grand Rapids: MI: Baker.

Van Brummelen, H. (2009). *Walking with God in the classroom* (2nd ed.). Colorado Springs, CO: Purposeful Design.